Praise for *My Three Friends*

Written with unconditional love, Eddleston has captured the lives of four little girls whose time-tested friendships have lasted through tragedies and triumphs, resulting in a chronicle of sweet memories and authentic descriptions of life's challenges. Within the book resides the tenderest gift life has to offer: to love and be loved for a lifetime.

> *-- Kelley Jacquez, author of Hiding Women and Other Stories of Acceptable Madness, a Southwest book of the year, 2014, and named one of the Great Books of the Year, 2013, by Madison Smart Bell, book reviewer for the New York Times*

I appreciated the logical, easy storytelling, the reminiscing of good feelings and the recounting of historical events.

> *-- Rick Burnham, retired elementary school teacher*

Eddleston has written a book that not only chronicles her life within her loving circle of friends, she has written a book that anyone who grew up in the 1950's and 1960's will delightfully relate to. And she has done it with humor, humility and wisdom. A marvelous trek down the best of memory lane!

> *-- Sally J. Jones, retired Director, Columbia 911 Communications District and published poet*

My Three Friends

MY
THREE
FRIENDS

Linda Eddleston

Alan,
Thank you for your
Wordfest leadership and
your writing inspiration!
Linda Eddleston

Karen Bonaudi, Ink.
Renton, Washington

My Three Friends
Copyright © 2015 Linda Eddleston

ISBN 978-0-9891430-2-8

Cover art and book design by
Poouster Graphics
Castle Rock, Washington

FIRST EDITION 2015
Published by
Karen Bonaudi, Ink.
www.karenbonaudi.com

Printed in the USA
National Color Graphics
Spokane, Washington

Dedicated in memory of

Rod Eddleston

Table of Contents

PART IV: OUR ADULT YEARS

Acknowledgments

Writing a book can be a lonely process, but not if the writing is a true story about friends. As I wrote these stories, the book became a path of shared memories.

Thanks to my dear friends Marilyn, Patsy, and Nancy for their enduring years of friendship and for allowing me to tell our stories.

My writer's group consisting of fellow writers: Mary, Marianne, Connie, Margaret, Donna, and Sally helped to encourage my endeavors. Our meeting times provided time lines for me to continue my progress.

Our community writer's group, "WordFest" is another source where writers and listeners meet to share their stories. Thank you to Alan, our leader, and to other faithful members who give helpful comments about our work and often purchase our local author's books.

Family (parents, siblings, and relatives) support started when I was young. This family branch has extended to my grown children and to my grandchildren. Their reassurance has always been my inspiration and purpose for writing.

Thanks to my editors Patsy, and Kelley, plus several others that gave me feed-back. I also give my heartfelt thanks to my daughter Selena, who understands the computer world.

This book is dedicated to my late husband Rod. He helped with research and often listened and gave insight as I slowly progressed in writing these memories.

He inspired me with his "can do" attitude to keep on task.

Preface

It took a long time to write this book. I've been working on this book for eight years. That doesn't mean that every minute of the those eight years I was typing at my computer, not even every day of those years, not every week, but mostly every month I added a section.

During these years I've structured sentences, reworded phrases, researched information, and completed scenes. For eight years I contemplated about it from the first idea to the editing, reediting, reediting, reediting, and reediting - and you get the idea.

When I started these chapters it wasn't about me. Well, really it was about me, but I changed the names. I had two characters and I called them Jeanie and Joan. Jeanie is the name that I wanted my mother to name me, instead my older sister named me Linda. Joan is Patsy's middle name. Patsy is the second character in my book. So the stories were about Jeanie and Joan. Then as the chapters unfolded I realized that I am Jeanie and Patsy is Joan. I could step in and be myself and I could call Patsy by her real name. Then I was deeply involved and the past became my present reality. That's when I brought my other friends Marilyn and Nancy (real names) into the story.

Every time I wrote about these memories, I wasn't in the present year (whatever these last eight years were) rather I was in the fifties, sixties, seventies, eighties, or the nineties. At times I was a child gathering chestnuts, a teenager having a conversation with my mother in the kitchen, or a student back in college staying up all night and studying for finals.

I lived this book for eight years. My goal was to write a story that I felt compelled to write. I had an idea that long lasting friendships matter. I realized that how we maintained these friendships over a period of fifty years despite difficulties, distance, and differences was worth sharing.

Did the book completely follow my vision? No, it took a life of its own. Did I feel inspired? Yes, I did. Did the finished book surprise me? Yes, it did. Am I excited to share these stories? Yes, I am!

I wrote this book like many scenes on a stage. The curtain goes up and there are two young girls trying to string two tin cans from one house to another so they can have their private telephone. Close the curtain and reopen it to another scene of neighborhood children entertaining their families with an amateur talent show, and then in later chapters, see two women friends walking along a beach path with one husband in a power wheelchair rolling beside them. Learn that he only has months to live, but they are outside enjoying the ripple sound of the river waves, feeling the warmth of the sunshine, and pretending all is well.

Read the post notes of what happened after the story events. Then share the discussion questions at the end of the book. Tell about what it was like when you were a child. Reminisce about your teenage years, your first date, and how you felt when you attended a high school dance. Share how children entertain themselves today and accomplish creative rewarding projects. Think about your adulthood friends and how you relate to them and their families.

Writing this book was worth eight years of labor. Now it is time to share these stories. This volume of memories, "My Three Friends", will take you on a noteworthy adventure.

PART I

OUR
CHILDHOOD
YEARS

The Tangled Mess

Marilyn and I were different. I loved school. She tolerated school. Gym class and recess were her favorite parts of the day. I hated recess. Reading and writing was what I enjoyed the most. Even as early as third grade, Marilyn thought of ways to get hall passes and escape from the classroom. I thought about a future career in teaching.

Since kindergarten we'd been friends and classmates at Sabin Grade School in Portland, Oregon. In third grade, 1954, we had the same teacher. One afternoon in science we heard about an experiment that captured even Marilyn's interest. Our teacher, Mrs. McSweeny, explained to us how sound waves vibrated and how these currents crossed through wires to make telephones and radios possible. She suggested that if two paper cups were strung together with a tight string, sound waves would vibrate through the string.

Marilyn sat across the classroom. I looked at her. She looked back. We both nodded. This was definitely a homework project to try.

As we walked home from school, (she only lived one block and I lived two blocks from school,) we talked about this possible invention. "Wow! This is so neat," I said. "We can actually make our own walkie-talkies!"

Marilyn had a serious look, "You know what, Linda? With a string phone we can talk to each other any time, day or night, and our parents won't even know."

When we got to her block, I started to run toward my house. I turned and yelled back, "I'll change my clothes, and meet you back at your house."

I was anxious to get started. The warm, crisp, fall weather felt like summer was over, but still lingering. I was dressed in a skirt and

2

blouse, saddle shoes and white socks. It wasn't a school uniform; it was just common school clothes. Our play clothes were pedal pushers, tops, and tennis shoes.

We decided to string the "phones" from her house, on Seventeenth Street to my house on Sixteenth Street. We also thought it would be wiser to use a tin can rather than a paper cup; after all, a paper cup would break apart during the first rain storm. So as soon as I got home, I searched in our kitchen for an empty tin can. My parents didn't save cans so I decided to empty a can of peaches, eat some, store the rest in the icebox, and then wash out the container.

I ran upstairs to my bedroom and quickly changed my clothes. As I ran out the back door, I yelled to Mom, "Bye, Mom, I'll be at Marilyn's."

Mom, who was downstairs washing clothes, yelled back, "Linda, did you change from your school clothes?"

"Yeah, Mom, see you."

When I got to Marilyn's she had a can ready too.

I came with a kite spool, and she brought a ball of string that her dad used for fishing. We decided to use the kite spool.

"Okay, now." I was ready to begin and started to give directions, "Somehow we have to punch a hole in this can and pull the string through."

Marilyn said, "That's easy." She ran down to her basement to find a hammer and a nail for punching a hole. When she came back, she quickly hammered her nail in the tin. The hole was rather large for the narrow string, but we decided we could make a knot around the side of the can and it would be fine.

3

I took the hammer and nail and made a smaller hole in my can. I didn't tie my string because we had to make our sting stretch from her back yard to my bedroom window.

Her bedroom window was on the ground level, so that wasn't a problem. Going across her backyard was easy, but then we decided we couldn't lay the string on the ground. So we looked for other options. There was one big tree in her backyard. Earl, Marilyn's older brother by five years, had carved bark steps into the side of the tree. There was a wood-framed pigeon coop already built in the tree, so this was the perfect perch for our telephone string. Earl didn't want any girl being up in his pigeon coop, but we considered this an exception to all rules, and if Earl was home, even he would understand our reasons for being in his special place. We did hesitate though about which one of us should climb up the tree.

"Climb up the tree, Marilyn, and throw your can over one of the branches."

"Why don't you climb up the tree?" I was surprised that Marilyn suggested that I climb the tree when she usually she was the daring one.

"Why me? It's your brother's pigeon coop."

"Okay," Marilyn agreed. "But, I already broke my arm once, and if I break my arm again, my mom will kill me."

That was true. Marilyn's arm cast had been removed only a few weeks before. She'd broken her arm by falling off the bunk bed. At the time, she was trying to throw something at her brother and leaned too far over the top bunk and landed on the floor. Of course, Earl yelled at her that her arm wasn't broken; however, she knew that her arm wasn't supposed to be all twisted like it was and hurt like it did. She had to tell her mother. She didn't want to face her mom with troubling news again.

I tried to reassure her that this time we were safe.

"Don't worry; I'll be down here to break your fall."

Marilyn still looked worried as she started to climb up the tree. "Great, then we will both have broken arms."

Finally, I saw the can hang down from one of the wooden boards that were braced across the branches. "I'll get it." I yelled.

I ran to the side of the tree and jumped to reach it. Marilyn climbed down backward until she was near the ground, and then she jumped down.

"You did it." I gave her a pat on her back. "Now all we have to do is get this string across Mrs. Hall's back yard, then across the street and up to my bedroom window." I gave these directions as we untangled the string and tried to pull it tight.

As soon as I said the words, I realized we had a hard task before us. Our time was limited too. I wanted to get this project done before my dad came home for dinner. I had the feeling he probably would not approve of our experiment, even if it was printed in a science text book.

We were familiar with Mrs. Hall's back yard, but we had only been there when Mrs. Hall was home. Mrs. Hall was a kind lady that helped me once when I was three years old. I had fallen on the cement stairs near our driveway and cut my forehead. My forehead was so badly injured I needed stitches. My dad had to rush me to the hospital. My mother was busy caring for my new born brother, so Mrs. Hall held me on her lap on the way to the hospital. She also held towels on my forehead while my dad quickly drove across town.

Often she and my mother would visit while standing on the driveway. Her only family was an adult son that lived at the coast. Knowing how kind and friendly she was we weren't too concerned about going over her five-foot cyclone fence. We also knew that she was at the coast for the week, so there just wasn't time to ask her if it was okay to go through her backyard. Her yard was like a small forest with several large fir trees and a koi fish pond. Our plan was to get our phone line above the fish pond and over one of the tree branches.

We looked around for the best tree. Finally, I decided I could climb up the cherry tree. It didn't look hard, and I figured I didn't have to climb too high. I hung onto the thickest branches and carefully stepped on one limb after the other.

I was up several feet when I yelled down, "What do you think, Marilyn, is this high enough?"

"Sure," Marilyn answered. "Just throw it over the branch and climb down."

I lowered myself and jumped off the lowest branch. We pulled the string tightly toward the front yard of Mrs. Hall's house. All of a sudden the string wasn't straight, but tangled and even knotted in places. I looked at Marilyn like it was her fault. "How did this happen?" I asked.

Marilyn looked upset, but didn't say anything. She took the string and started to walk backwards so we could pull the string between us. Then I started to unweave the mess and unknot the knots. I couldn't help it, but I started to giggle, thinking how hard this project was becoming. Marilyn did not laugh. She was tackling this project seriously. Every time we moved we had to be careful not to wrap the string around ourselves. Finally it was straight and tight again.

Then we faced another problem. We had to get the string phone across the street. We sat on the curb and wondered how to hang our string cord in the air over the street. We knew that laying the cord in the street was not a good idea because, even though it was a rather quiet road, cars would come and run over our phone line.

We sat for several minutes discussing possibilities. Then we had the same idea at the same time. The can phone will have to go over the telephone wires. I didn't think that was a problem and neither did Marilyn. All we had to do was toss our can over the wires.

Throwing a can that high was more of a challenge than we first thought. Marilyn tried tossing the can again and again. Finally, I had an idea. If we stood on Mrs. Hall's porch (her porch was high on a grassy slope) then maybe we would be high enough to get the can over the wires. Sure enough, Marilyn's baseball practice came in handy, and she was able to toss that can high in the air. Over the wires it went. Now all we had left to do was get that can and pull it toward my garage. I knew I could climb onto our garage roof from our side yard; it was a trick I had done before, after watching a wild cat climb up to my bedroom window. From the garage roof, I would have to leap over the cement walkway below and land on the house roof.

As we planned our next move, my father came home. Usually I was happy to see my dad coming home from work; this time I wished he would have waited until we had finished our project. He saw us in the street staring up at the telephone wires, the hanging can, and the long string.

He came over to us and stood in the street looking skyward, and mumbled, "Well, Linda." Then he paused. He always spoke slowly as if he was thinking before he said his words. Then he asked, "What's up?"

"Hi Daddy, our can is up. See, we're making a telephone that Marilyn and I can use to talk to one another. We read about it in science today!"

Dad put his hand on his head and flattened his dark hair as if that would help him think. "Well, I hate to tell you this, but you have to take it down."

I pleaded with Dad, "Why, do we have to take it down? We haven't even tried it out yet!"

Dad was firm, "Sorry, gals, but you can't have string and a can going across telephone wires."

He headed toward the garage. Marilyn and I just stared at our all day project and realized that our goal was going to fail.

Dad came out with a ladder and a pair of scissors. In the middle of the street, he placed the ladder in an upright position. He told us to tell him if a car came by. He climbed up the ladder, cut the hanging string, and caught the flying can.

As he climbed down the ladder, he told us we'd have to gather up the loose string that we had in the neighbor's yard and get ready for dinner.

Marilyn and I looked at each other with total sadness. Now we shared a shocking realization that we couldn't even try our string phone to see if it worked. This unsuccessful experiment ended any interest in future joint, science projects.

******

Patsy moved across the street when I was five years old. I felt, at the early age of five, that this new girl coming into the neighborhood would disrupt my life. So, instead of giving her a warm welcome, I displayed my worse childhood behavior. Our first meeting was more like a territorial battle than a pleasant experience.

The Unwelcomed Greeting

The first day Patsy and I met, we did not greet each other nicely. She was six years old. The year was 1950. She had moved into my neighborhood with her mother, father, and younger brother. I lived with my mother, father, and younger brother across the street from Patsy.

We lived in Northeast Portland. Though Portland was a busy city, we lived in a quiet neighborhood. Yards were divided by bushes and driveways rather than fences. Most of the roads were paved and there were cement sidewalks. Between our houses there was a side street called Mason Street; it was unpaved and rarely used, so it was easy for us to cross the street and visit often.

The day we met, she stood on her corner, and I stood on my corner, shouting back and forth. My first call was a bragging statement, "I have a nicer house than you do."

She answered back, "No, you don't. Our house is nicer than yours."

I repeated my first statement, "My house is nicer, so there!"

Patsy paused for a moment, and then asked, "How do you know? You probably haven't ever been in our house."

"Yeah, I have. I was in your house before you moved here."

Patsy answered back, "Yeah, well, we've painted some rooms so you don't know what it looks like now."

Maybe they did paint some rooms; however, I knew the difference between her house and my house. My house sat on a high grassy bank with a huge front porch. It had a big living room. Also, we had an extra side yard. Her house was on the corner lot, but it sat lower. It had a smaller porch and a backyard with no side yard.

I was quick to yell back, "Well, it doesn't matter anyhow 'cause I've lived here longer than you."

Patsy shouted back, "Well, I know more than you know 'cause I went to a better school 'fore comin' here and I'm smarter."

"No, I'm smarter 'cause I've lived here all my life and I know all the neighbors that you don't know."

Patsy thought for a while and then yelled back, "I know about a lot of places 'cause I've been 'round most of the world. My dad's in the Army, and we've been to more than twenty states. How many states have you been to?"

I thought about it and knew that besides Oregon, the only other states I had been to were Washington and California. I didn't even know the names of most other states, but I answered, "I've been to lots of states too."

Patsy was quiet. Then she announced, "I was born in Georgia!"

I thought, Wow! Georgia sounded like an exciting place to be from. I was born in Portland, but that really didn't seem like a fun place since we were in Portland, so I lied and named the only other state name I knew. "I was born in Texas. So there!"

I sat on the curb and she sat on her curb across the street. I found a stick and played in the dirt. I watched a caterpillar crawl over my stick. There was complete silence. I was happy with my announcement. It felt good to think that I was born in Texas, even if it really wasn't true.

Then we heard Patsy's mother calling her.

Patsy looked at me and said, "I have to go, Mom is calling me for dinner. My name is Patsy. What's your name?"

I told the truth this time. "My name is Linda"

Patsy started to run to the house. Then she turned and yelled, "Do you want to play tomorrow? I have lots of dress-up clothes, and we could play make-believe at my house, if you want to."

"Sure!" I quickly answered. "That sounds neat. I have one long blue satin gown. I wore it at my sister's wedding." Then I bragged, "I was a flower girl! I will wear it tomorrow and show you. See ya' 'morrow. Bye."

She stood up and ran toward her back door, screaming, "Bye and adiós."

I didn't know what "adiós" meant. Maybe she did know more stuff than I did.

*****

Patsy and I spent time devising clever, creative play ideas. Our mothers were at home busy with household duties. They trusted us and depended on us to go outside and amuse ourselves, so most of the time we played at my house or at Patsy's. There were a few times, though, when our projects took us beyond our yards.

You're in my Yard

The neighbor's yard was overgrown with ferns and bushes and surrounded by a wooden fence. From what we could see, we thought that this neighbor was never at home. All we knew was that he went to work and lived alone. We never saw him talking with the other neighbors, so we didn't think he was all that friendly. Yet, we climbed over some broken boards on the lower part of his fence and stopped to make friends with his barking terrier dog, who ran toward us, giving us a welcome greeting rather than a warning. Then with the dog's permission, we made our way across the yard and trampled over the green fern plants.

Suddenly, the front door of his house swung open. A rather fat man with messed up light brown hair, wearing a partly-opened smoking jacket and loose-fitting bedroom slippers, stomped across his wooden front porch yelling, "Hey you're in my yard! What are you girls doing?!"

Patsy and I nervously looked at each other. We had discussed for a long time whether we should even go into this yard. We knew almost every neighbor for several blocks. We played with other friends further down the hill, and our parents knew the older people that lived up the road, but we didn't know this man.

He yelled at us once again, only louder this time. "What are you gals doing?"

I shouted my reply, "We're gathering chestnuts, Sir."

It was early fall 1955. We were doing one of our favorite activities, adding to our chestnut collection. Even though Patsy was a bit taller than I and a year older (she was ten and I was nine) I usually spoke up first because Patsy often hesitated. She took time to think carefully before she spoke. I didn't like long silent pauses.

The owner stepped off his porch and walked closer to us. He stared at us. We were dressed casually, almost identically, with flowered blouses, pedal pushers, and white tennis shoes. Both of us were tall and thin with long blond hair. Often we were mistaken for sisters because we were always together and frequently dressed the same, whether or not we discussed it before hand. For this project, each of us carried a large, brown, grocery sack.

Sounding doubtful, he rephrased my answer, "You are picking up chestnuts?"

"Yes," I firmly repeated, even though the truth could mean more trouble. Not only did we trespass, we were also stealing his chestnuts.

The man took a glance around his grassy lawn. His yard was covered with chestnuts from his huge tree. He had a mean look, as if seeing the numerous nuts made him angry. Obviously, he didn't appreciate the chestnuts as we did. As he moved in our direction, he slowly pronounced each word and asked us, "Why are you gathering chestnuts?"

Again I was quick to reply, "Because they are pretty." We had gathered chestnuts from other yards, but his yard had the most chestnuts. We liked finding these reddish smooth nuts. After we collected them we sorted them in separate piles and we counted and recounted them. We had quite a collection, but we wanted more. Having chestnuts gave us a successful, rich feeling. We knew they could be eaten, but cooking them and/or eating them wasn't part of our plan.

Now we were face to face with someone who might spoil our fun. The man stared at us. There was a long silence. Patsy and I stood there in fear of his next move. We waited. He glanced around his yard again. I wondered, would he tell our parents or just yell at us and chase us off his property? I could feel my stomach aching.

"Hell, I'll pay you for picking up chestnuts. Fill up your bags, and then I will pay you each a quarter."

Patsy and I looked at each other surprised and happy. Patsy seemed completely amazed. As soon as he turned his back and headed toward the house, she whispered to me, "Linda, do you think he really will pay us?"

I didn't hesitate; I just turned and yelled toward his direction, "Thank you, Sir."

Patsy and I started to giggle. We couldn't control our laughter. We felt so giddy. We were overjoyed to be rewarded for our effort and not scolded. Never did we think we could get paid for picking up chestnuts. This was like having an opportunity for a future career. Someone was actually going to reward us for doing something we already liked doing. It was a good day.

*****

A new girl moved into our neighborhood. Her name was Nancy.

Innocent Phone Calls

Nancy was a friend who came from clear across the country, a southern state, where they spoke differently - Arkansas. When she moved to our neighborhood, back in 1955, she was the only student in our class, that I knew, who lived with only one parent. Her parents were divorced.

She knew her father and had memories of him, but they were limited recollections. A Navy man, living on a ship, he was seldom home. Since the divorce, he wasn't around at all.

Nancy lived in an apartment with her mother. Her mother worked full-time, often during the evening shift. Nancy, at the early age of eleven, was fairly independent. After school and during the evenings she took care of herself.

As our friendship grew, Nancy spent more time with my family. Often, she ate with us, even if we went out to dinner. My family did not have a TV set, so after school Nancy and I had a habit of going to her apartment to watch the "Mickey Mouse Club Show." We especially liked seeing the continuing episodes of "Spin and Marty."

One late afternoon, Marilyn joined us and we took advantage of the fact that Nancy's mom was not home and we were unsupervised. We were fifth graders at the time. We decided to try several prank jokes. Randomly, we called numbers from the phone book. Then, when someone answered the phone, we asked them questions.

"Hello. We are taking a survey. Can you tell us please, is your refrigerator currently running?" Most people would answer, "Yes."

"Well, if your refrigerator is running, then you better hurry and go catch it." Then we would hang up and laugh uncontrollably and make another mischievous call. We did this several days in a row. We had numerous gag jokes. They were all fairly innocent riddles, but someone that we called didn't have the same sense of humor, and they reported us.

I didn't know at the time, but I heard these details later that even back then, the authorities were able to trace our calls. I also heard that a police officer came to Mrs. Spencer's (Nancy's mom's) apartment. From what I heard, I could imagine the scene:

"Hello, are you Mrs. Spencer?"

"Yes Officer, is there a problem?"

"May I come in?"

Mrs. Spencer opened the door for Officer Jones. "I reckon you can, come on in."

Officer Jones got right to the point, "Is your phone number ATwater-2-2760?"

"Yes sir, Officer that is correct."

"Well, there have been prank phone calls coming from this number, disturbing several residents, and they have submitted these complaints." Then he handed Mrs. Spencer a list of recorded phone numbers, dates, and times.

She was shocked. "There must be some mistake. Only my daughter and I live here and I assure you I'm not making prank calls."

"Then it must be your daughter."

Mrs. Spencer was quick to deny that. "She wouldn't do anything like that."

The officer knew what kids might try. "You are probably right. Acting alone she probably wouldn't do something like this, however, if she was with friends, they might have made some prank calls just as a joke, mind you, for the fun of it. You can see the dates and times the calls were made."

She sat down and then carefully looked at the list. Suddenly she came to the realization that the list included times when Nancy was at home but not always alone.

She stared directly into Officer Jones' eyes and firmly stated with her southern ways, "I'm fixin to make sure this won't happen again. No more a larking, mischievous pranks 'round here. No sir, this won't be happenin' again."

That satisfied Officer Jones. "Thank you, Mrs. Spencer. Have a good day."

That same afternoon, when the police officer called on Mrs. Spencer, and I came home from school, my mom met me at the door. "Linda, you are to go straight over to Mrs. Spencer's house. She wants to talk to you, Marilyn, and Nancy."

I questioned my mom, "Isn't she at work today?" This was very unusual because Mrs. Spencer seldom missed a day of work.

"No, she had to stay home today and she wants to talk to you girls now." Mom emphasized the word now.

I could guess what this conversation was going to be about. I felt nervous and guilty, and I feared the worst. I tried to reason with myself. It wasn't entirely my fault. I actually tried to discourage Nancy and Marilyn from making the phone calls. But I didn't stop it. I went along with the plan. I laughed at the jokes like they did. So I was guilty too. We really didn't have a clue that anyone would report us or that it was even possible to discover our secret tricks. I figured that since my mom knew what we did, Mrs. Spencer probably had told Marilyn's parents, and we were all in trouble.

When I got to Nancy's apartment, Nancy and Marilyn were already sitting on Mrs. Spencer's couch. They looked guilty, like how Adam and Eve probably looked right after eating the apple. Mrs. Spencer told me to sit down. Then slowly, in her southern drawl, she declared, "Now girls, I called y'all together 'cause I need to talk to y'all. I hear tell that y'all been making annoying phone calls to strangers! This ain't okay. A police officer actually came to my home today and informed me that these calls came from my phone during the same hours that you' all were here. Now this will stop and it never will happen again. I reckon you understand. Do y'all understand?"

Marilyn started to defend us. "We wouldn't do that."

Nancy and I stared at Marilyn with a You-better-admit-the-truth-and shut-up look.

Nancy lowered her head and quietly mumbled, "Yes, Mom, we understand."

Marilyn knew she was defeated; together we echoed, "Yes, Ma'am."

Then Nancy added, "We're sorry, Mom. We were just having some fun. We weren't saying any bad things, or anything like that, we were just saying some jokes on the phone."

Marilyn and I added our apologies, too.

We were sincerely sorry. Mrs. Spencer sighed in relief. We knew, kind of, that the confrontation was over. We got the clear message we were not going to play phone tricks again.

Patsy, Marilyn, and Nancy were my closest friends. We also knew almost everyone else that lived within three to five blocks of our neighborhood. There were several children that were either younger or older. Often we all had times of playing together. One day I got an idea that ended up including the entire neighborhood.

The Big Production

In my backyard, Patsy and I practiced tumbling lessons on the grass with an old mattress as our gym mat. In detail, she explained to me how to do a proper cartwheel. "Put your hands in the air and reach for the sky. Place your right foot in the direction you want to go." While explaining, she demonstrated in slow motion: "Place one hand on the ground, one foot in the air, push and kick, place your other hand on the ground and while keeping your legs straight up, kick and swing your body over. See. It's easy."

I was close to success, but not good enough. Patsy took tumbling lessons and she was very flexible. I didn't take lessons and felt awkward. Attempting a flip, the splits, or a back bend caused me pain.

If she held my back, I was able to lean over her arm backwards and get into a spider walk position. My hands were flat on the ground, my elbows pointed to the air, my feet were braced on the grass, and my knees bent pointing upward. I could arch my back and in this upside down position walk like a spider. I felt this was impressive because few other children, let alone adults, could do the spider walk.

All of a sudden, I had an inspiration. "Why don't we have a talent show? We could do our double somersaults, and you could do cartwheels."

Patsy didn't answer. She just kept flipping her body and doing one cartwheel after another. So then I added another thought. "You could sing. You have a nice voice, and I could play *Hot Cross Buns* on the violin."

I received no response. While she was doing tumbling rolls, my mind was rolling with images. "We could ask Ronnie to play the flute." Ronnie was Patsy's brother.

I still didn't get a reply. Her body just kept flipping from one stretching exercise to another contortion. She was not taking me seriously. Often I had ideas that seemed so brilliant at the time, but then I didn't always follow through. Like for several summers in a row I rehearsed the play *Cinderella*, with me playing the lead role. I had all the lines memorized and I wore my blue satin gown, but we never did perform the play.

This new idea made me excited, and I wanted Patsy to join my ambitious plan, but she wasn't sharing my enthusiasm.

I continued. "I think it would be fun to get others to be in our talent show, too."

Patsy stopped her tumbling. She sat on the mat, looked at me, and then asked, "Linda, who are you talking about?"

"I'm talking about other kids in the neighborhood. We could all be in the show. Let's see there's Marsha, Miriam, Marilyn, Nancy, Janet, Raymond, even Donald down the street, and the twins, Leslie and Lisa. Everyone could do a talent and we could invite all our parents to come see the show. Parents love to see their kids perform."

Patsy finally showed some interest. "And where would we have this amazing talent show?"

"On my front porch." It seemed so logical. My house had a huge front porch. On some days my porch was my pretend classroom, other days it was my play house, and now it would be our performance stage.

That evening Patsy and I sat on the porch steps, with paper and pencil, and jotted down our ideas. I started some suggestions. "Marilyn could play the clarinet."

"Yeah," Patsy agreed, "Didn't she play a piece at the school assembly?"

"Yeah, and I played with her on the piano.

"That's right; you did."

"But I can't get the piano on the porch so if she plays that piece, she will have to play alone, which is okay because she had the melody anyway."

I kept adding names and possible talents to share. Marilyn could sing beautifully, but it took a lot of begging to get her to sing. I didn't know if I was up to begging that much.

Nancy was taking accordion lessons and her mom had recently bought her a new bright red 120 bass accordion. I was envious. I was sure that I could get Nancy to play a piece on her new accordion.

Miriam, who was two years older than we were, got straight C's at school (C's were the highest grades - the other grades were S's and N's - which meant satisfactory or not satisfactory) so Patsy and I decided she could maybe do a reading. Then we had to decide about Raymond and Donald. I had no idea what they did well. Oh, I forgot about little Susie. She would also want a part. At the age of three, it was hard to decide what she could do. Saying a nursery rhyme would probably be best.

Then there was Darrin, the daredevil kid. He would do anything we asked him to do. He once climbed the walnut tree to nearly the highest branch. He would ride his wagon down Eighteenth Street, straight down that steep hill without stopping. One day, when the neighbors weren't home, he even jumped off their garage roof, landing on a dirt pile. Of course he did these tricks because we dared him to and he did them away from his parents' eyes. What could he do that would be a safe trick for parents to witness? We would have to ask him.

22

That evening I told my mom about our plans. She was all for the idea, though she warned us that some parents might not come. Mom explained that some fathers worked late, or into the early evenings, so they might not be able to attend our show.

Mom said we would need to serve refreshments. "You can't invite all these people here without serving food."

I hadn't thought about food. Having food meant spending money and we did not have any money. That's when the idea came that our guests should pay for this show. If we sold tickets in advance, we would have enough money to serve refreshments.

It was early June 1955; we decided to have the performance in late August. We had a busy summer of making tickets, programs, posters, planning and preparing every day for the upcoming talent show. We were committed.

We gathered the kids together and talked about the upcoming production. We did listen to their ideas, but mostly we told them what we wanted them to do, except for Darrin. He had a terrific trick in his mind so we decided he could do whatever he wanted.

The day before the program, Marsha and Miriam decorated the front porch with crumpled crepe paper and balloons. Patsy's mom and my mom made cookies, and Marilyn's dad, who was a baker, made a flat, two-layer cake, decorated with frosted musical instruments and the words, "The Big Talent Show."

Patsy and I were pleasantly surprised because every parent bought a ticket to this upcoming event. At five cents a ticket we had collected $1.50. With that money we bought seven Kool-Aid packages for three cents each package, napkins for ten cents, paper cups for twenty-five cents and a gallon of ice cream for fifty cents. We had forty-four cents left over. Even though it wasn't enough extra money, my mom took the forty-four cents, gave it to my dad and sent him to the store to buy more ice cream.

23

Finally, the night of the big production came. Of course, I assigned myself as hostess for the evening. I looked at the audience. They were seated on their own lawn chairs that they brought for the occasion. Their chairs were placed in a row on the grass area in front of the stairs to our front porch. The porch made a perfect stage. Their seats were somewhat crowded together but, they each had a good view. I looked at their faces.

I knew everyone that was there. I took a deep breath. I told myself to keep breathing and just do it. Then in a loud, bold voice I shouted, "Ladies and gentlemen we welcome you to the first talent show of Northeast Irvington Neighborhood. I'm sure you will enjoy the entertainment. To begin the evening, Ronnie Walker will play his flute piece, Swaying in the Breeze, a tune he composed."

Ronnie was a natural at music. He played the piece without error, at least it sounded good, but since he made it up, we wouldn't recognize if there was an error or not.

Marsha and Janet came on stage next. They were dressed in matching poodle skirts and sang, *How Much is That Doggie in the Window?*

Miriam did a reading from the story, *The Little Prince*. She was an excellent reader and everyone was quiet and attentive. Marilyn played a solo on her clarinet. Nancy played, *William Tell* and *The Beginning Polka Waltz* on her accordion.

After that song, I announced a short intermission. It was a perfect warm evening, about seventy-six degrees. Everything was working out so well, and yet I was so nervous, my stomach ached. I could not even look at the refreshments, let alone eat anything. It was hard to keep the performers on the side of the house. We needed a closing and opening curtain, which we did not have.

The next acts needed the music from my record player so I plugged it in with an extension cord and told the audience we would begin again soon. The song Irish Fling started to play. Leslie and Lisa came on stage. Using individual jump ropes, they skipped to the music, and did several tricks. They twirled their ropes over their heads and tossed the ropes in circular forward and backward movements. Their feet were doing front cross, leg-over cross, and the single side swing. They ended with quick jumps as the music got faster. Everyone clapped loud because Leslie and Lisa did a great job; they also looked twice as cute, because they were twins.

Raymond played *America the Beautiful* and *You're a Grand Old Flag* on his trumpet. Next, Susie, looking very small and beautiful in her pink dress and long blond ringlet curls, sang her ABC's and told the nursery rhyme story, *The Three Little Kittens Who Lost Their Mittens*.

Donald came on stage and told a story called *The Three Bears*, but not the original version:

> *Once there were three bears: papa bear, mamma bear, and baby bear. Their names were Shut-up, None of Your Business, and baby bear's name was Trouble. One day Trouble got lost. Mamma and Papa Bear looked everywhere. Finally, they asked a policeman for help to find their baby cub. The policeman agreed to help. First he asked Papa Bear, "What is your name?"*
>
> *Papa Bear said, "Shut Up." The policeman was shocked. He looked at Mama Bear and asked in a firm voice, "What is your name?"*
>
> *Mama Bear answered, "None of Your Business." Now the officer was really mad and he asked, "Are you both looking for trouble?" And they replied, "Yes!"*

I was concerned, wondering how our parents would react to this joke; however, they laughed and clapped, and Donald bowed.

25

Then I did my violin solo. Despite my nerves, I only made one mistake. Next, Patsy brought out the mattress. Everyone had to turn their chairs to watch Patsy perform her tumbling tricks on the grass. She did cartwheels, stood on her head, and ended with the spider walk. Then our audience turned their chairs toward the stage again.

Darrin marched up the stairs onto our stage. He wore a black suit and a tie, and gray tennis shoes. He announced, "Today you will see a trick that has never been performed on this stage before." I thought to myself this has never even been a stage before. He continued, "I am going to stick a pin through a balloon without popping the balloon." Then he took a flat, white balloon out of his pocket. He blew the balloon up and tied a knot on the end. Then he showed off his balloon by walking across the stage and raising the balloon so everyone could see. Then he took a straight pin out of his other pocket. He showed everyone his pin. Then very slowly, he stuck the pin through the top of the balloon. It did not pop! Everyone was silent and looking at Darrin. He took out another pin out of his pocket and slowly stuck it into the side of the balloon. Once again he held the balloon up for everyone to see. It had not popped! He looked at the audience and said, "To prove to you that this really is a balloon and my pins are really sharp I will take one more pin from my pocket and..." Then he poked the pin into the other side of the balloon, and with a loud pop, the balloon pieces flew every direction. The parents clapped and yelled, "Bravo, bravo!"

Then all the kids came on stage to take their final bow. Everyone stood and applauded. We remained standing and sang the first verse of *God Bless America*.

The parents and the kids gathered around to eat the treats. Raymond's dad started talking about how good our talent show was and about having another performance. "Hey, Raymond, what do you think about doing this over again, and doing it at our house?"

A few months later, they did just that. I didn't organize the second talent show. Donald and Raymond and his dad did the work for the second showing. In Raymond's back yard they built a wooden platform stage. They used a shower curtain for a stage curtain and even had flood lights! It was in September, right after school started; they did an early evening performance. I repeated the violin solo. I enjoyed being part of the audience. This time I ate several cookies and drank a tall glass of Kool-Aid.

*****

One day, Patsy and I decided to go on an adventure. We wandered further than we had planned. The end result turned out more drastic than we expected.

Adventure

It started out to be an innocent adventure, but it became a worrisome incident that prompted our fathers to think about whether or not to involve the police. The day was inviting, warm and sunny. It was one of the first spring days after many cold, rainy winter days, in Portland. The temperature was seventy-six degrees. The warm sun rays gave us extra energy. Patsy, age ten, and I, age nine, were planning a day of exploration. The year was 1955.

We knew about the nearby Water Tower Park, but we didn't go there often. That park had playground equipment and swings, but we had heard about a terrible accident that happened years ago. There was a haunting memory of a child losing his life at that park. The story was that a boy had climbed up to the top of the water tower, in the middle of the park, and fell from the tower to his death. Since that incident, a high chain linked fence was built around the obstacle, yet every time we went to the park we often would think about the image of the boy falling off the highest tower rim. It never seemed like a pleasant place to play.

Strawberry Hill was a place that gave us a sense of a remote getaway in a city neighborhood. It was called Strawberry Hill because it was a grassy knoll with a dirt path and wild edible berries growing amongst the tall surrounding weeds. Often we sat on the dirt path eating unwashed berries we picked off the vine. It was there we had our private talks.

Our Sabin School grounds, only two blocks from our homes, was another recreation site. The school play area was equipped with monkey bars, parallel bars, (where we would hang upside-down and do chin-ups), and a merry-go-round. The merry-go-round had wooden benches that were held together with iron bars. We'd sit on the benches and hang onto the bars while one or two kids ran and pushed the merry-go-round and then jump on board. Sometimes we were more daring and leaned our bodies back, and held our arms in the air.

28

We enjoyed the breeze as we circled around. This contraption was dangerous. Many children scraped their knees landing on the cement ground from falling off this miniature carousel. Other times they fell by tripping over their feet while pushing the merry-go-round. Still, it was popular.

On this particular Saturday, it seemed like the ordinary activities were not enough. We wanted a day of adventure. So we each packed a sack lunch and told our busy mothers that we were going for a little walk and we'd be back soon. Patsy's mom added goodies to her lunch bag. My mom was hanging up wet sheets on the clothes line. She heard our idea and just said, "You girls have a fun time and, Linda, be back before your father gets home."

We knew our limitations. Even though we lived only a block away, on Sixteenth and Mason, crossing busy Fifteenth Street was a definite "no, no." Fifteenth Street was a two-lane road, full of traffic and it had a city bus route. Also, many Negro families lived on the other side of Fifteenth and we had been told not to go over there. The message to me was, "Negro families would not be happy if we were in their neighborhood." I thought differently.

I actually knew differently. One day I did cross Fifteenth, with a colored friend from school named Dorothy. Dorothy and I were good friends at school. We joked around a lot and played together during recess time. The day came when she invited me to her home. I didn't know exactly where she lived, but I said, "Okay." So after school we walked to her house across Fifteenth Street. When we got there her house was full of family members. Her mother offered us snacks. Her father, sister and brother all welcomed me.

Later, I told my dad. He told me to remember not to go across Fifteenth Street and he reminded me that the Negroes didn't like us and even though it seemed like they did, they didn't. Well, in my mind, I disagreed. I also understood that I would not disobey my father. I accepted the fact that Dorothy and I would probably never be close friends outside of school. I also knew for sure that we liked each other and that her family liked me.

So, with this one street restriction, we strolled down the Fifteenth Street sidewalk and avoided crossing the street. Within ten blocks we arrived at Fremont Street. There was a corner drug store that had a soda counter. They sold candy, gum, pop, and if we were really rich, milk shakes. Near the front of the store was a comic book section, where we read books as long as we wanted without purchasing anything.

Usually, my friends and I did not go beyond this corner store, but today was a day of adventure, so Patsy and I kept walking. We watched the squirrels running from the oak trees, we heard other children playing in their yards and we felt some cool water spray as we walked by a man washing his car. The air smelled of fresh, cherry tree blossoms and a mixture of gas fumes from the road.

We arrived at the busy intersection of Knott Street; beyond were the fields of where Lloyd Center would eventually be built. There we sat amid the tall grass, eating our packed lunches. Patsy's mother had fixed her a peanut-butter and jelly sandwich, carrot sticks and home-made chocolate chip cookies, which Patsy shared with me.

I had made myself a Miracle Whip and lettuce sandwich, which was a little soggy from being carried in my paper bag. I also had two bananas, one that I shared with Patsy. We had nothing to drink and we didn't see anywhere to get a drink.

Hours had gone by, but the day was still clear and beautiful. Patsy asked, "Linda, have you ever walked across the bridge to downtown Portland?"

"I thought about it and said, "No, but my family and I watched the Rose Festival Parade several times on the Burnside Bridge."

"Well," Patsy hesitated, but then with excitement added, "let's cross the bridge."

"Okay," I answered. I never was one to stop an idea that included more activity. It seemed too early to head back home.

So we continued walking. It was more walking than I anticipated. Riding in a car across the bridge is a different experience than walking across the bridge. Near the end of the span was the homeless mission. We became very aware of the bums sitting on the curbs and lingering on the sidewalks. Some were even lying in the shade of the building's shadow. A few of them were obviously talking about us as we passed by. We kept going and no one bothered us.

It was after we crossed the bridge, we discovered the Skidmore Fountain on First Street. This was a fountain built in the middle of a main street on a cement circle platform. We splashed the cool water through our fingers and laughed as we playfully splashed each other. We used our hands as cups to drink from this sink pool of refreshing water. We read the inscription: "Built in 1888 by Olin Warner, funded by Stephen Skidmore for the purpose of giving drinks to horses, men and dogs." As I finished reading aloud, I laughed and added; "Now the fountain is giving drinks to us!" I felt like we were part of history.

I suddenly realized that we had been gone a long time, so I told Patsy, "We better head back because if my dad gets home and starts wondering where we are, I could get in trouble."

Patsy's dad was slightly easier going than my dad. We weren't too concerned about her parents, just worried about my dad's reaction. So we decided we better not wander the streets of downtown Portland. Instead, we focused on heading back across the bridge and returning home.

Walking back took longer than going. We were tired. The thrill of seeing something new at every corner was gone. We also had the worry of getting back home before dark. These frustrations took the joy out of our hike.

Despite our rush to get home, we made a slight change from the way we had gone. We went a few blocks out of our way to see Benson, the all-boys high school, a place we wanted to explore. While we were looking at the campus of the school, we heard our names being yelled, "Patsy, Linda, get over here this minute!"

What a surprise to see our fathers together! It was amazing that they actually found us, as we were still several miles from home. Now we had to face both of them at the same time - it did not look good. We knew we were a lot farther from home than we should have been, even if wandering areas were not previously clearly defined.

Mr. Walker started the scolding with the question, "What were you girls thinking?"

My dad continued the questioning, "Do you know you've been missing for the last six hours?"

They really didn't give us a chance to answer. It didn't seem like six hours, and we didn't know we were missing.

Dad continued, "Both of your mothers are sick with worry."

I couldn't visualize Patsy's mother ever being upset. I didn't think my mom would be too concerned; she always seemed too busy with her housework. I just couldn't imagine her worrying about my whereabouts.

Then, in agreement, they added the last surprising statement, "We were ready to call the police."

We didn't commit a crime. Did they think we didn't know our way home? We were safe, we knew where we were, and never once did we think we were lost. I remember wondering, what was all the fuss about and how many miles did we actually go? I just wanted to dwell on the exciting feeling of enjoying a fun day of adventure.

*****

We didn't know it, at the time, but Patsy would soon be on another adventure, only not with me, but with her family.

You've Got To Be Kidding

Patsy did her usual morning ritual. I heard the shrieks outside my upstairs bedroom window. From the street below, she sang, "Stodole-pump, pump, Stodole-pump, pump." These words were from a Czech folk song. Patsy's dad played the accordion and sang German and Czechoslovakia songs. These song lyrics told the story about a frog croaking at a barn or water pump. The words stuck in Patsy's mind and she often repeated this musical phrase.

It was Patsy's way of waking me up in the morning. I didn't like hearing my mother call me in the mornings and I hated alarm clocks, but having a friend yelling from outside my window - that was different. I would hop out of bed and quickly get ready. This morning was a Saturday so I wasn't eager to answer her call.

I stood on my bed to reach the window ledge. I opened the window. Looking over the roof line from my upstairs bedroom window, I saw Patsy below on the street. I opened the window slightly and yelled back, "Why are you shouting at me on a Saturday morning? I don't have to get up today."

"Well," Patsy was eager and alert, "It's nine o'clock and I've got some news to tell ya."

I leaned further out the window, "Can't it wait till ten o'clock?"

"No, it's urgent." Then Patsy gave an order, "Throw on some jeans and come on down."

Patsy usually wasn't a demanding person, so I decided this must be some important news.

"Ok," I sighed.

I ruffled through my pile of clothes on the dresser seat, and found my cut-off jeans. I slipped my jeans on, pulled a pink tee shirt on and slid my feet into my thongs. I took one quick look in the mirror and decided I better put my long straight hair in a pony tail. I felt around on the dresser and found a rubber band. Then I took both hands and smoothed my hair back. With my left hand I held a wad of hair and with my right hand stretched the rubber band around the strands. Now I looked much better. I ran down the stairs, and without saying a word to my mom who was in the kitchen, I ran out the front door.

Patsy was sitting on our front porch steps. I stood over her and asked, "Ok, what is so important it couldn't wait till later?"

"Well, I have some really exciting news so sit down and listen."

I reluctantly sat down on the cement steps; my lazy weekend was going to begin an hour before I was ready. "Okay," I said, "I'm ready, and this better be good."

"It is good news. My mom is having a baby and we are moving!"

I sat there thinking how could her mom be having a baby? My mom wasn't having a baby, nor did I think she would ever have another baby. Patsy and I had younger brothers close to the same age. I also had an older sister, but she had already moved out of the house. Patsy and I were only one year apart, and it didn't make sense to me, that now her family would be so much different with a younger child. Also, the idea of her moving didn't make sense at all. Patsy had only lived across the street for three years. People didn't move into houses and then quickly move away. My family had lived in the same house since I was born, and I was ten years old; they weren't talking about moving anywhere. Last of all, Patsy said this was good news; there was nothing good about Patsy moving away. She was one of my best friends and lived across the street. How could it be good for her to move away?

I figured I had heard the message completely wrong. "What did you say?"

Patsy repeated her exact words in slow motion. "My mom is having a baby and we are moving."

"Why would your mom have a baby? Where are you moving to?"

At the time it just seemed rather odd that there would be changes. The other troubling question I had was how was I going to survive without Patsy being near? I even depended on her to wake me up in the mornings.

Patsy tried to reassure me. "Don't worry we are not moving that far, just a few miles away. Maybe you could ride your bike to our house. I'll tell you all about it."

She stood up and used hand gestures to describe in detail the new house, really an older house that would be new to her family. "We are moving to the Alameda District. The house is big with a large back yard. It is a two-story house. I will have my own bedroom upstairs. It is so neat, Linda, I even have a low ceiling walk in closet, like a hidden play room."

I was beginning to get interested. "How does the yard look compared to your yard?"

"This is the great part - it even has a tree house, though Ronnie already claimed that spot as his." I agreed the tree house really was going to be off limits.

"Oh yes," Patsy continued, "There is an attic in the house, and the people who lived there before left all kinds of interesting stuff. We could dig through the trunks up there and look at some of the clothes, pictures, magazines, and books."

I visualized Patsy and me exploring this new house, running in her back yard, walking the streets, and riding our bikes exploring the neighborhood. Maybe, it wasn't going to be the end of our friendship. It would just be a little harder. I was determined that Patsy would still be my best friend.

I asked the painful question. "When are you moving?"
Her answer was like a dart hitting my heart. "Mom said we will be moving in a couple weeks."

*****

Nancy impressed my parents. Whenever she came to our house or went out to eat with us, Nancy thanked them repeatedly. "Thank you so much. It's so kind of you to take me to dinner. Can't I pay for my meal? Really, I would like to pay y'all for the dinner. Well, thank you. I really had a great time and thank you so very much."

Of course, she never had any money to pay for her dinner, but she would offer. So my parents always said that Nancy could come along. One summer we invited her to come to Camp Colton with me for a week of summer camp. I was hopeful for a happy week, but it turned out there was to be one extremely sad incident.

Could This be True?

I felt great. The air was crisp and cool. The gentle breeze made it feel refreshing compared to the stagnant heat of Portland. I loved looking up at the clear sky. No matter where I stood, I could stare upward into the tree branches encircling the camp. I enjoyed the mint smell of the evergreen trees. The day was warm. I could feel the sun rays heating my bare arms and legs. It was August 1956, the summer between our fifth and sixth grade school years. I was excited to be back where I felt comfortable, at Camp Colton. This was Nancy's first camp experience.

My parents, Nancy, and I had completed the fifty mile drive from Portland to Camp Colton in Colton, Oregon. After checking in at the registration desk, I was anxious for my parents to leave. I wanted to show Nancy our cabins, the dining hall, the dirt hiking trails, and the fire pit. This was going to be a whole week away from home with boys and girls our own age; it was like freedom in the semi-wilderness.

At the time, I had no inkling that during the middle of my camp week, I'd feel quite differently. There would be a day when I would call home and beg my parents to come back; however, as my parents were leaving, I couldn't imagine such a need. I mumbled a fond, but speedy good-bye. "Yeah, Mom, I got my tooth brush. Yes, Dad, I love you. Of course, I won't go swimming without the lifeguard on duty. I know, Dad, 'Don't get lost in the woods.' Don't worry we won't wander too far. Yeah, we'll have a great time. Write. Yes, we will send you a card too. I love you... Bye ...."

Finally, my parents' two-toned yellow and black, 1951 Mercury drove over the gravel path and out through the log gates and away.

I begged, "Come on Nancy, I want to show you the cabins." We each grabbed our luggage, rolled up sleeping bags and trudged down the path to the last cabin back in the fir trees.

Nancy checked out our new living arrangement. She looked disappointed, as she looked at the rustic wooden cabin. "This is it?"

"Yeah," I replied. "Isn't it great?"

"Great? There is nothing here but wall-to-wall bunk beds."

I had to admit it appeared rather quiet, dark, and bare. There was evidence of other girls claiming their spots with their sleeping bags, pillows, and suitcases on the beds as if they dumped their stuff and left quickly. They were either exploring the rest of the camp or already at the lunch hall.

I looked around the room to see if I could add a positive comment. "And open air space at the top of the wall covered with glass windows." Then I corrected myself - "Covered with only screens."

Nancy was searching for electric wall outlets. "I suppose we don't have a TV or radio anywhere."

"No, Nancy. Remember we are here to learn about God and the Bible, not to be entertained."

She glared at me, "Fine, Linda, but where do I plug this in?" Nancy had opened her suitcase and pulled out a curling iron.

"Nancy, there isn't any electricity in this cabin, not even light switches. See!" I pointed to the bare, wooden board wall to emphasize my point.

"Then how do we see?"

I opened my suitcase and pulled out my flashlight. "That's what this is for." I demonstrated by shining the light rays of my extra-large flashlight over the wall of the cabin.

"Actually," Nancy sighed, "there isn't much to see anyway."

"Come on." I started to walk out the back doorway. "I'll show you where we wash up in the morning." I led her to the wooden back porch where there were rails and shelves. On top of the shelves were white tin basins and a row of faucets. I turned on the faucet. I let the water drip slowly over my fingers. "See, all we have to do is turn on these faucets, and fill the basin with nice...cold water." I remembered, from being at camp before, that the water never got warm. It would always be cold.

Nancy's next question was, "Where are the mirrors?"

"We don't have mirrors."

"How are we supposed to know how we look?"

I realized then I should have brought a mirror along. I looked at Nancy. She had short dark curly hair. I had long straight blond hair. She was as tall as I was, taller than most girls our age. She weighed a little more than I did; I was too skinny. She had a nice figure, and I thought she was cute. Her complexion was clear. Her facial features were rather small. Her eyes were narrow and blue. I had wide, blue eyes. On her teeth were braces, but she still had a cute smile. "You look great" I replied.

"Sure, now I look great, but how will I look tomorrow?"

"Don't worry, we will get plenty of sunshine, you know, and we'll be tan. Tomorrow we will look even better."

Nancy frowned, "Burnt and dirtier. Great." Nancy was not a positive camper, and this was only our first hour at camp. I trusted that soon she would enjoy camping. Then the fun would begin.

"There is a pool." I added. "We can go swimming tomorrow."

"Do they have mirrors at the pool?" she wondered out loud. I couldn't remember if they had mirrors there or not.

40

"Okay, what about the toilets? Where do we go to the bathroom?"

I knew this would be the hard part for Nancy to accept. I spoke quickly hoping she wouldn't concentrate on the issue. "The toilets aren't far, just down the dirt path. Just be sure that you take your flashlight and wear your shoes."

"Linda, you've got to be kidding. You didn't mention anything about outhouses."

"You didn't ask."

It was close to 12:30, and I knew we were supposed to be at the mess hall. "Let's hurry so we can meet some of our cabin mates."

Nancy was combing her hair with her left hand and using her right hand to unpack her suitcase. Then she started hanging clothes on some nail hooks. We had already selected the bunk bed that we were going to share. She chose the top bunk and I accepted the lower one. I didn't see any rush to unpack. "Come on Nancy, let's go." I grabbed her arm and started to pull her out the door. I knew she wanted to check a mirror before we left, but that wasn't an option.

"All right, all right I'm coming!" She yelled as I kept pulling her along.

The dining room was a long log cabin. In rows there were wooden picnic tables and benches. On one side of the room sat the boys and the girls sat on the other side. Kids were already sitting on the benches waiting for announcements and for lunch to be served. Every table had a sign. Our assigned table was named "Naomi." Naomi was the name of our cabin. All of the cabins were named after Old Testament Bible characters. There were five girl tables and five boy tables. The boys' tables were named Noah, Abraham, Daniel, David, and Solomon. The girls' tables were named Ruth, Esther, Naomi, Marion, and Sarah. I knew by the end of the week we would learn details about each one of these Bible characters.

41

We found a spot to sit. We had just swung our legs over the bench to sit down when everyone starting singing, "Announcements, announcements, annou-ounce-ments!" It was a signal to hush and listen. The camp director got up first. His name was Mr. Chuck. He was the leader last year, too.

"Welcome everybody! Are we going to have fun? I can't hear you? What are we going to have this week?" The kids all yelled back "Fun," then louder "FUN," and then they spelled it out "f-u-n!" Chuck had his guitar and started to play. While he played, he shouted into the microphone, "How many of you know your states?" Most everyone raised their hands. "Where are you now?" He sort of yelled and sang the question.

Some kids yelled Camp Colton, but some yelled Oregon. Then Chuck started singing, "Where has Ore-gon boys, where has Ore-gon, where has Ore-gon boys, where has Ore-gon? I ask you now as a personal friend, where has Ore-gon?" Then he pointed to the boys' side of the room and he expected a singing answer.

After a few minutes of confusion the boys sang back. "We don't know, Al-aska, we don't know, Al-aska. We don't know Al-aska. We tell you now as a personal friend, we don't know Al-aska."

The girls responded back with "She went to find her Ne-bras-kee, she went to find her Ne-bras-kee. I tell you now as a personal friend she went to find her Ne-brass-kee."

Mr. Chuck stopped singing and took time to introduce all of the cabin leaders. He told us that after lunch we would be able to sign up with our leader. Our choices for the rest of the afternoon would be hiking, creek-walking, crafts, or playing volleyball. I knew that my favorite activity was creek-walking. I loved following the rocks along the creek and feeling the cold water swiftly run between my toes. Tomorrow the pool would be open and that would be my choice. I saw the crafts displayed on one long table. There were a few things

I wanted to make during the week, especially one beaded cross necklace. I looked at Nancy and pleaded, "Let's sign up for creek-walking." It was important that on this first day we did everything together. The next day we would probably meet other friends and our hours would not always be spent side by side.

We sang the Doxology Song for our table prayer and then we started to eat. Surprisingly, it was one of my favorite foods, hamburger sandwiches with lots of ketchup, potato salad, which I just passed to the next person, and potato chips. I drank two glasses of cold milk. I also made sure that I got two chocolate chip cookies, saving one for later.

There was one previous year at camp that I had a bad meal experience. It was during breakfast. They served the one breakfast food that I hated, hot oatmeal, or as I called it "mush." Even though my dad ate mush every morning, I would never even try it. It looked awful to me. So when they served it at camp I didn't try it there either. There was one camp counselor who had the attitude that every child should "at least try a bite of everything." So she approached me that morning and suggested that I at least try it. Of course, I absolutely refused. So she suggested that I sit there on the bench in the dining hall until I did try a bite. I knew that I could sit there all day and all night. It didn't matter to me, I would not try mush. So I sat there. She eventually got tired of waiting for me so she told the cleaning crew that I could leave when I tried a bite of my mush. The time went by and I just sat there. It was getting to be near noon and the lunch crew wanted my space so they said I could leave. Other than that experience, all my times at Camp Colton were of good memories. I was hoping that my camp meals would all be pleasant and that there would be no more breakfast problems. I didn't know it then; but I would have an upsetting experience, though not a food issue.

The evening camp fire was always the best time. There was a Pastor who spent some time telling us Bible stories by the camp fire. Then there was singing. "Do Lord, O, Do Lord, O do remember me.

Do Lord, O, Do Lord O do remember me. Do Lord, O, do Lord, Do remember me, Way beyond the blue. I've got a home in glory land that outshines the sun..."

The singing went sometimes until ten o'clock. I loved evening campfires. I was wide awake at ten o'clock. When the fun time ended, we used our flashlights to find our way back to our cabin. I tried to go to the bathroom early in the evening so I could avoid late night trips in the dark. I didn't want Nancy to know, but I wasn't very good at roughing it either.

By the light of our flashlights, and some large flashlights that our counselor brought, we brushed our teeth, changed our clothes, and snuggled down into the warmth of our sleeping bags -- after we brushed out the brown sugar that some boys had secretly put in our sleeping bags.

By the next day Nancy and I became good friends with two other gals in our cabin named Karen and Paula. We became a foursome. Every day we decided together what we would do. If the four of us didn't join together, at least two of us would be doing the same activities.

It was on Wednesday, in the middle of the week, that something upsetting happened. Even though I had these close friends with me, I felt alone. We were sitting in the chapel during a Bible study. I was looking at the front of the hymn book that was placed on the pew rack. There on the first page was written: "This hymnal is given in loving memory of Gilbert Franklin Rose." I froze with fear. This was my father's complete exact name. Though I knew in my head that my father was alive and well, my heart sank as if the words were real. It was ridiculous, I knew, but I was feeling physically ill. Everyone started to sing, "Fair-est Lord Jesus, Rul-er of all na-ture ..." I couldn't sing. I could not stop my tears. I just wanted to sob.

Nancy saw my reaction and asked me what was wrong. I couldn't explain to her. Pretty soon our counselor Miss Brown asked me what was wrong. I started to cry harder and told her I just had to leave. She walked out the chapel door with me. I kept crying and did not explain to her why. Then I begged her to let me call home.

Finally, she relented and stopped asking me questions. She took me to the dining hall. There was a pay phone on the wall. I told the operator I wanted to make a long distance phone call to Portland. I gave my number BE 4008. I heard the operator's voice, "Will you accept a long distance phone call from a Linda Rose?"

My mom's voice gave a firm "Yes." I tried to compose myself. I really didn't want to upset her. "Mom, I want to talk to Dad."

"Linda, what is wrong?"

"Nothing's wrong, I just gotta talk to Dad."

"Well, your dad is at work. What do you need to tell him? Is everything all right? You sound upset?"

I sighed, just hearing Mom's voice did reassure me that everything was the same and dad was okay, but the sick feeling was still lingering. "I'll call later, Mom, when Daddy is home. I love you. Bye."

The counselor looked at me with a questioning stare. Still I didn't give any details that explained my outburst. I knew that I would not calm down until I heard my dad's voice.

The rest of the camp day I was sad. Though Nancy tried to comfort me, I still wouldn't tell anyone why I was so upset because I knew it was foolish.

That evening I called home again. Dad answered the phone. I just sobbed, "Daddy, I'm homesick and I want to come home."

He tried to reason with me saying that I was only going to be at camp a few more days. Still, I continued my pleading and begged him to come get me. Finally, Dad gave in and promised that he and Mom would drive up the next day.

I went to bed still uneasy. I just had to see and hold my dad. I couldn't believe it myself. The week had been going so well, even Nancy was enjoying camp. I was making crafts and swimming, and creek-walking. I was having a grand time until that moment when I saw the name in the hymn book. It was too real to ignore. I needed the proof of seeing my dad strong and healthy.

True to my dad's word, by five o'clock the next day my parents arrived. I ran to the car to greet them. Dad got out of the car looking tall and muscular. He hugged me and I knew everything was all right. I smiled and said, "Thanks for coming, but I'm fine now I don't need to come home till Saturday."

Mom gave that puzzled irritated look, like why did we come all this way just to turn around and go home. But, Dad smiled and said, "Well, I'm glad you're okay."

They stayed for our dinner meal. Then we said our good-byes. Nancy asked me, "What was that all about?"

I answered, "Nothing much, I just wanted to see my dad."

I ran down the path singing, "I have the joy, joy, joy, joy down in my heart, down in my heart, down in my heart ...."

*****

As my grade school years came closer to ending, I became very worried about high school. I depended on my friend Patsy to help guide the way.

What Will I Be When I Grow Up?

I decided to be a teacher mostly because of the influence of my third grade teacher, Mrs. McSweeny. She was a kind lady, of average height and weight, usually wearing a nice flowered dress with low heeled shoes. Her auburn hair was curled and pulled neatly back, not in a bun, but held with hair pins to the side of her face. Her smile was continuous and she always demonstrated a patient manner.

Even though we were third graders, we had a resting time while she played "The Brahms Lullaby" on the piano. It was during third grade we were introduced to cursive writing. Although it was a stage of being very young, it was also the beginning to being more independent learners.

One day, around October, she announced to us that near the end of the school year we would be going on an all-day field trip exploring our downtown city of Portland. School was fun that year. My goal was to be in third grade for the rest of my life, if not as a student, then as a teacher.

My best friend Patsy had not chosen her future career, yet I thought Patsy would make a great teacher. She liked learning type of games. With a deck of cards we played the game called "Authors." It was like playing the card game "Go Fish." Our game was with pictures of famous authors and a list of their most popular classical books or poems. I would ask her, "Do you have Sir Walter Scott with the book title, 'Lady in the Lake'?"

Then she would answer, "Yes," and hand me the card or answer "No" and ask me a question. "No, but do you have Alfred Lord Tennyson with the title, 'Charge of the Light Brigade'?" From playing this game over and over I learned many author names and book titles long before I got to college and studied English Literature.

During the summer of 1959, I had just finished eighth grade, Patsy had completed her freshmen year. I was scared to death of high school so she acted as my mentor. I wondered, "How am I going to make it through high school?" I sat outside in our lawn swing swaying back and forth enjoying the heat of the sun and the soft summer breeze when Patsy ran up the driveway. Dressed in summer shorts, short sleeve blouse, and her long blond ponytail flipping in the air, she ran toward me. Then she showed me a package wrapped in brown postal paper that had just arrived in the mail.

"Oh, Linda, look what came in the mail this morning. Get some scissors and let's open it."

I ran into the kitchen and by passed my mom as she was busily heating the wax paraffin on the stove for canning strawberry jam. I dug through the messy junk drawer and found the scissors. I didn't even talk to Mom. It was best when she was busy to just walk by or she'd be asking me to hand her something or to remind me of some unfinished chore.

I hurried back to Patsy, "Here are the scissors. What did you order in the mail?"

I had never ordered anything from a catalog so I was very curious about the whole process, let alone what was in the package.

While Patsy un-wrapped the parcel she talked about how much fun we were going to have working on this new exciting project.

Patsy and I enjoyed doing lots of creative things together so I imagined new dress up clothes, a board game, a creative art set or a dangerous science kit. I was surprised and slightly disappointed when finally, the wrapper opened enough that I was able to see the label on the box, "You Can Remember! A Home Study Course in Memory and Concentration" by Dr. Bruno Furst.

48

It sounded more technical than what I was able to handle. It certainly did not sound like fun, but Patsy was extremely enthusiastic. With gusto, she started to read out loud the instruction manual.

"If you went to the grocery store and forgot your grocery list could you remember the items you needed? After you practice the methods taught in this kit you will never have to write a grocery list again. You will be able to recite from memory the items you need."

I still wasn't too impressed because I wasn't worried about grocery lists at all. My parents didn't even write lists they just went to the store at the spur of the moment and got what they needed. Patsy continued summarizing what the kit was all about.

"Be the student you want to be, amaze your teacher, and be at the top of your class. Use this kit to help you to learn about geography sites, memorize arithmetic facts quickly, spell your words correctly, and even recite the capital cities of the world without referring to a map!"

Then she read word for word what this memory course had to offer:

"If you really do the exercises presented in these sessions, you will almost immediately experience a definite improvement in your memory. Step by step, forgetfulness will become a discarded bad habit, and proficiency in memory and concentration will take its place.

You, like all human beings, have the two attributes which are the most important aids in the process of improving your memory. These are the ability to form mental pictures, and the ability to associate such pictures with each other."

"See Linda," Patsy continued, "if we practice these simple steps, in no time at all we will be smart - we'll be able to memorize lots of trivia"

I wasn't even sure what the word "trivia" meant, but I was excited about being the student at the head of the class rather than at the back desk wondering what was going on. "Okay." I relented, "What are these simple steps?"

Patsy acted as my teacher. That day we practiced all the steps starting with three words and using numbers to associate with word lists. Then we memorized the model grocery list.

We learned memory tricks that I used through high school and college days and even later. As it turned out, it was a good preparation course for my future.

*****

The last party at Sabin Grade School was the eighth grade dance called the "Friday Frolics. Though the evening was disappointing in some ways it also became the initiation of my interest in the male population.

Friday Frolics

"Hey pretty gals, what's your names?"

We stopped our bicycles and started talking to three boys on their bikes. Nancy was quick to answer with her southern drawl. "I'm Nancy and this here is Marilyn and she's Linda."

"Where are you going?"

"Oh, we all just rid'ng round."

"You live around here?"

The cutest boy kept asking the questions.

"Well, not exactly we all live near Mason Street. Marilyn lives on seventeenth, Linda lives on sixteenth and I live on fifteenth."

We always had this little joke my dad was a butcher, Marilyn's dad was a baker, Nancy's mom was a waitress, not a candle stick maker, but it started out with the truth and the same as the nursery rhyme. Thank goodness, Nancy didn't mention that embarrassing rhyme.

"What school do you go to?"

Marilyn answered this time, "We go to Sabin."

The talkative boy answered back, "We go to Grant High."

I responded back, "Really?" They looked younger than high school age.

Marilyn bragged, "In the fall we will be freshmen too!"

This comment prompted another boy to add, "We're sopho-mores."

The boys kept circling their bikes around us the whole time as they were talking. We stood holding our bikes. The street was a fairly quiet side street with no traffic.

One boy was rather short with a dark crew cut. He kept doing tricks with his Schwinn bike, lifting his handle bars in the air until the front tire was off the ground and then jumping high over the curb. We heard another boy call him Jeremy.

The other two boys were taller than we were. One had red hair and lots of freckles, but still he had a cute face. He answered to the name Patrick. The one I immediately liked, was rather quiet, but smiled all the time. He had long blond hair, not long to his shoulders, but long enough. My parents would probably say he needed a haircut. He was tall and thin. He actually introduced himself and he looked directly at me and said, "Hi, my name is John."

I noticed his bright blue eyes. "I'm Linda, nice to meet you John."

"Well, Linda, have you been to any of the high school dances?"

I hadn't been to the high school and certainly not to a high school dance. Then, before I could answer, Marilyn blurted out, "Next Friday, Sabin Grade School is going to have the eighth grade Friday Frolics."

The boys kind of laughed about the name and made a sarcastic remark, "Wow, the Friday Frolics, sounds like fun."

John winked, smiled and seriously said, "Who knows we might show up." Flirting with Nancy, Patrick made teasing remarks about Nancy's Arkansas accent and kept asking questions about how she could have a southern drawl if she lived in N.E. Portland. Jeremy started demonstrating all the different ways he could ride his bike with no hands on the handlebars, no feet on the pedals and even while sitting backwards on the seat.

We laughed. We enjoyed being entertained by these goofy teenage boys. All of a sudden I realized it was almost five o'clock. "We've got to leave. I'm supposed to be home before my dad comes home." We were by the Alameda district about a mile away from our Irvington neighborhood.

My dad wasn't one to fear, but one to respect. Often he was our means of transportation, taking us places like the movies or ice skating at Lloyd Center and then afterwards he would come back and treat us to hamburgers and milkshakes at Yaws. So when I said, "I had to be home before my dad gets home," Marilyn and Nancy didn't argue. We got on our bikes and started to ride.

I heard John yelling as we were leaving, "Well, we may see you later."

Nancy yelled back in her usual flirtatious way, "Great meeting you all. Bye."

Up to this time in my life (eighth grade) my parents trusted me. I freely roamed the neighborhood, going places with my girlfriends. My mom was always busy with housework and preferred to clean without my brother and me being in the house and messing up while she straightened up. She was quick to give me permission to go places.

My dad was different. He wasn't always home, but he expected his wife and kids to always be at home. Whenever I asked to go places his first response was, "No."

Going to the Friday Frolics was no different. His initial reaction, even though it was a school function, would probably be a no. Marilyn and Nancy were going and I wasn't about to stay home on this night even if I didn't really know how to dance.

Previous weeks, Marilyn spent time teaching me how to do the basic Four Step, the Hand Jive and the Stroll. I thought I had "The Stroll" down pat. I thought the "Bunny Hop," another popular dance, was stupid; however, if there was a cute boy dancing, then I was prepared to hop around the gym while hanging onto his back.

After begging my parents all week, and using whatever psychology techniques I could devise, I finally got permission to go to the dance as long as I followed my parent's restrictions. I was to be home by 9:30 p.m. I wasn't to leave the school grounds until the dance was over. Then Marilyn, Nancy and I were to walk straight to our homes. The school was only one block from Marilyn's house and we always watched each other walk the next block so it was a very safe passage back home. I agreed to all the stipulations.

Marilyn, Nancy and I spent several hours planning what we would wear. Finally we had it settled. I chose my poodle skirt with a hoop stiff petticoat. Nancy wore one too. Marilyn thought those skirts were rather ridiculous so she wore a plaid reversible skirt. Wearing matching white blouses, and saddle shoes with white socks, we felt cool and connected. I tied my hair in a pony tail with a rubber band. Nancy had short natural curls. She always looked cute even without wearing rollers at night. Marilyn's hair was rather short and straight, but she too added some side curls for this special occasion. We were nervous, giddy and excited.

Marilyn had been to several church dances. She was Mormon and they actually had dances at her church. I was Lutheran and some congregations said no to dancing, one belief I didn't see in the catechism or the Bible so I didn't totally agree; however, I also hadn't been to any dances.

Finally, the evening came. We went downstairs to the school gymnasium. The 45 RPM records were playing one song after another. When we walked in we heard the song "Stagger Lee." Very few kids were dancing. Mostly the boys were sitting on one side of the gym and the girls on the other. We sat on the wooden cafeteria benches on the side where all the other girls were lined up.

Toby finally came over and asked Marilyn to dance. Toby had been pestering Marilyn all year so it wasn't surprising that he asked. The only boy that had shown any interest toward me, at school was Ricky. Ricky was there but I knew he would be too shy to walk across that wide gym floor to ask me to dance. Though once, when no one else was around he even walked over to my house and visited with me on our front lawn.

After several songs they played "Sleep Walk" and started to do The Stroll. I was thinking, "I might get asked to do The Stroll now that I know how to do it." They were definitely lining up with boy and girl partners, but I did not get asked. So I sat on the sideline watching while Marilyn and Nancy did The Stroll with their boy partners. Then Nancy got asked again to dance with another boy named Gary.

I sat by the wall watching the clock hands move or not move. After drinking a glass of punch and eating several chocolate chip cookies I was feeling like it was time to leave. Then Ray Anthony's song, "The Bunny Hop" started. Marilyn and Nancy came over and begged me to dance, with them, in the long bunny hop line. So I did, although it wasn't my dream come true. There were no boys by our group section, only girls hanging onto one another hopping in a long line. I tapped my right foot two times, my left foot two times, hopped forward, hopped back and then three hops forward right to the beat of the music.

Marilyn and Nancy were invited to dance again so I went back to my seat against the wall and watched the clock as they played one of the last slow songs, "Smoke Gets in Your Eyes." I was feeling like tears were getting in my eyes. At last it was nine o'clock, and time to leave. Marilyn and Nancy were laughing and kidding around about their great evening. I was disappointed. I figured I could cry about it later when I got home.

Just as we left the gym, we saw our three friends riding their bikes around the school playground. John even had a light on his bike glowing in the semi-darkness. As soon as they saw us, they raced in our direction.

They said that they tried to come to the dance, but the teachers guarding the doorway, wouldn't let them because they were high school students and didn't go to Sabin.

We started to pair off. Jeremy said he had something to show Marilyn and he took out a bag of marbles from his pocket. Patrick was already busy talking to Nancy and pushing her on the school merry-go-round. John and I sat on the back school steps.

John seemed so nice. We started talking. It was easy talking to him, as if we really knew each other. I asked him lots of questions about what it was like to be in high school. I was scared to death of high school and how different it would be to change schools. Sabin had been my school since kindergarten. I walked to school every day and some days even came home for lunch. I couldn't imagine what it would be like to go to different classes every period, to take a bus to school every day and have homework every night. I wondered how I could possibly ever pass a high school math class.

I didn't tell John all my concerns, but he made high school sound like lots of fun. He bragged to me about all of the things he had made in his shop class. Then he talked about how he liked his math class, and he counted to ten in Spanish, saying he learned that in his Spanish class. His accomplishments were very impressive.

We sat there talking away when we noticed it was getting darker and the school flood lights came on. Marilyn and Jeremy were over on the side of the building. It was getting rather quiet over there. Could they be kissing?

John was holding my hand. I was having too much fun to even think about what time it was.

Then, all of a sudden, off in the distance, I heard my dad call my name. Then I heard Marilyn's dad call her name.

I slipped my hand away from John's hand, and stood up. "I've got to go and go quick. My dad is coming. See ya, bye." Then I gave him a warning, "Get your bike and leave."

He was yelling something like, "Can I get your phone number?"

I ignored his question and started running to where I thought Marilyn was. All I could think of was to get out of there quick. My dad was coming. Luckily, I saw Marilyn and Nancy coming toward me. I saw the boys grabbing their bikes and racing across the field into the darkness.

Then I heard my dad's voice. "Linda, why aren't you home? You were supposed to be home at 9:30. The dance ended over an hour ago."

I had no idea an hour had passed. It didn't seem that long. I couldn't believe it. Could it be almost 10:30?

Marilyn's dad had his car. Marilyn went straight home with him. Nancy and I got in my dad's car. He told us he was about ready to call Mrs. Spencer, and tell her that Nancy wasn't home. Nancy's mom was at work and that would have really upset her.

We were all in trouble. My dad started questioning. "What were you doing out there so long?"

"We were just talking to some school friends," I semi-lied.

"Well," My dad spoke slowly but firmly, "You were supposed to be home at 9:30. The dance ended. The school was locked up." Then he said something that he had never said to me before. "You are grounded!"

There was no time frame of how long I was to be grounded. I knew Dad was furious. I figured I'll be grounded till I'm twenty-one!

What a horrible way to start my high school days. I also knew that after this embarrassing evening I'd probably never see John again.

Yet, I secretly felt somewhat okay. I had a boy that liked talking to me. He even held my hand. He was cute and nice. I ended up enjoying the evening. I was glad that I got home late, and had that extra time on the playground, because I didn't feel great about the dance only about the meeting afterwards.

So I decided. "I'll wait. I'll be very good. I'll do lots of chores. I'll hope my parents forget that I was over an hour late and I am grounded."

*****

John wasn't the last high school boy that captured my attention. The next one I met at Grant High School.

PART II

OUR
TEENAGE
YEARS

My First Date

"Don't look now, but is that guy, over there, staring at me? Gee, Nancy, I told you not to look."

"Which guy are you talking about?"

"See, he's sitting alone at the end of the table. He's the cute guy wearing a blue shirt."

"Well," Nancy sighed, "How am I supposed to figure out who he is if I don't look?"

"Well, you can look. Just do it rather subtly. You know, move your head, toss your hair back, and then take a quick glance."

Nancy and I were freshmen at Grant High School, Portland, Oregon - 1959. We were walking through the lunch line. I grabbed my usual toasted cheese sandwich and chocolate milk shake. Nancy made her own salad fixings from the salad bar. She always watched her weight and tried not to overeat. I was never concerned about my weight. I was too thin and actually hoping to gain weight by frequently drinking milk shakes, though the shakes at school were so thick they were impossible to drink. I reached for a plastic spoon so I could eat my milk shake.

For the last two weeks I had been noticing this handsome guy staring and smiling at me. I had no idea who he was, but he definitely captured my interest. I always smiled, whether anyone was noticing me or not, so I was positive that he thought I was smiling at him.

Seeing him every day was making my lunch period much more interesting. I knew he wasn't a freshman. He was actually sitting at a table where mostly seniors sat. It was hard to believe that a good-looking senior would be staring at me, but it appeared to be true.

Nancy continued, "Okay, I think I know which guy you are talking about. He's cute, but I don't know who he is. He kind of looked away when I tried to look at him."

I groaned, "Oh dear, I hope he didn't think we were talking about him."

"Well, Linda why don't you just walk over there and ask him something."

"Like what? 'Hi, I notice that every day you're staring at me. Do you have something in your eye? You seem to be blinking a lot.' "

"No," Nancy paused to think. "Maybe, you could say, 'These chocolate milk shakes are really cool.' "

I thought about her suggestion. Then I said, "That sounds like something a freshman would say. Naturally, they're cool. More like freezing cold. No, I'm just going to wait and maybe he'll say something to me. Like, 'How about a date?'"

"That would be nice," Nancy added, "but I say if you don't say something nothing will happen."

Nancy was well versed with guys, flirting easily, and always knowing what to say. Sometimes Marilyn and I would get disgusted just listening to her playing up to the boys. One evening we met some guys that were stationed at the Navy Base. Even though Nancy's parents were divorced, Nancy actually had a legitimate shopping pass to the base because her father was in the Navy. We shopped all right. We went shopping to look at the guys. A couple guys started to flirt with us. Nancy got the attention of the cutest one. With her soft, southern slow voice, unlike her usual tone, she would drawl, "Oh, you work with radios - you're a radio technician! That is sooo neat. I just can't imagine how smart you must be to understand radio work. Tell me all about it." Every guy she met lapped it up like a cat with cream.

And like a tomcat, he would fall for her, get her phone number and call her the next day.

Marilyn and I were not as successful catching guys or getting dates. Marilyn liked the fellows, probably as much as Nancy did. I wasn't too excited yet about boys. I was quite content to stay home. I liked working on my scrap books, listening to my records, or just going out with my girl friends. Yet, seeing this handsome senior acting as if he liked the looks of me was encouraging.

Weeks went by and basically I only smiled at this mysterious senior. Then one day, after talking to Marilyn and Nancy about him, Marilyn told me that this admirer was Earl's friend.

I was surprised. Marilyn had a different lunch period than Nancy and I, so she really didn't know that this guy had been staring at me for so long, until we started talking about it and one day pointed him out in the hallway. "You know him?"

"Yeah," she answered, "Sometimes he comes over and hangs out with Earl."

"What's his name?"

Marilyn wasn't too excited about him. Anyone who was a friend of her older brother's didn't interest her too much. She answered, "His name is Norman."

I smiled, "Wow, his name is Norman, I like it!"

I didn't have any clue how to get beyond our simple smiles, his wink, and our casual "hi's" as we passed in the hallways, or when I saw him at lunch. He didn't seem to know how to get beyond that either. I felt rather hopeless. Then the day came when I actually had alone time with Norman.

I had taken the bus across town to NE Klickitat Street for my weekly piano lesson. I was standing at the bus stop heading back home to SE Portland when a nice looking guy in a red open convertible drove up to the bus stop. He asked me, "Would you like a ride?"

I smiled and looked at the car first and then at the driver. There he was, "grinning Norman." Here was my chance to get to know this admirer. I quickly said, "Yeah, thank you!"

As soon as I sat down on the front seat I commented on the neat car. I could see the blue sky and feel the breeze blowing my hair. I didn't care if my hair style changed, I was feeling great.

He asked me why I was catching a bus and where I was going. I told him that my family had moved to SE Portland, but that I was finishing my school year at Grant. I also told him about taking piano lessons back in my old NE neighborhood so that was why I was taking the bus. Then he told me that he was planning to go to college after high school, and that he wanted to be a lawyer. Between the red convertible and the attorney plan, I was impressed.

Then he really shocked me by asking if I would like to go to a movie with him on Friday night. He wanted to go to a drive-in with another couple and asked if I could go along. I gave him my phone number and told him I would let him know later in the week. I was thinking to myself, how can I get my parents to give me permission to go to a drive-in movie with a senior? Forget about asking my dad; he definitely would say no. I would have to beg and bribe my mom. I waited a couple days then I started the process.

"I cleaned my room, Mom."

Mom looked surprised about my announcement, "Good" she replied.

"I also got my homework all done, practiced the piano and cleaned out the bird cage."

"Great, now you can set the table for dinner."

I went to the silverware drawer, grabbed some napkins out of the basket on the counter, and started to set the table. "I met this guy at school. He's really smart. He's also very nice."

My mother just kept peeling potatoes without responding. "Anyway," I slowly continued, "I've been talking to this boy at lunch and he kind of asked me out. Like I said, he's really nice, and smart."

"Where did you meet him?"

Obviously, Mom was only listening to part of what I was saying.

"I met him at school. He eats lunch in the cafeteria the same time that I do. Marilyn knows him."

I was sorry I mentioned Marilyn because I would have to say he's one of Earl's friends. Earl was older and that would immediately tell my mom that Norman was older. I decided to keep going. "Marilyn knows him because he's Earl's friend."

"Hmmm," was all Mom mumbled. Mom was thinking.

"Anyway," I wanted to continue this conversation and not let Mom think too long. "He wants to take me to a movie with some other kids from school."

"Linda, don't forget the place mats." Mom was more concerned about the dinner plan than my quest.

She was making this rather difficult. Maybe I should have asked her after dinner, but I didn't really want her undivided attention, I only wanted her to say yes before she really realized the whole picture.

"Anyway, he asked me out for this coming Friday night and I really, really want to go. Could I go out with them?"

64

"Out with whom?'

"Mom, this guy at school that I met. His name is Norman. Marilyn knows him and says he's a nice guy. We see each other every day at lunch."

"How would you get to the movie?"

I knew now that Mom might say yes.

"He drives."

"Well, he's not a freshman if he is driving. What year is he?"

"He's a senior." There, I said it.

"A senior?"

"Yeah, Mom, but a really nice senior. He even told me he wants to go to college and become a lawyer."

"Well, that's fine, but you are only a freshmen and going out with a senior is a bit much for a freshmen."

"Oh Mom, he is really a nice guy and a very good student. I know you will like him. And we are going with another couple. We won't even be alone. We will come home right after the movie, I promise. Please, please."

"Which theater are you talking about?"

"Well,..." I hesitated to tell her this part. "He wants to go to a drive-in."

She responded just like I thought she would, "I don't feel comfortable letting you go to a drive-in movie with a guy who is a senior."

I responded back, "Not just any senior - a very nice, polite senior. Don't worry, Mom, we will be fine. Besides, we're going to see that movie, 'North by Northwest' with Cary Grant." Mom liked Cary Grant so I knew that was a convincing piece of information.

"Remember, Mom, you said, I should see that movie. You said it's really exciting and good."

"Yes, it is a good movie, but not at a drive-in."

"But Mom, that is the only place it is playing. When you meet him you will like him I know you will."

"Well, you know your father would not approve." Mom was reluctantly giving in.

"I know just tell him I'm going to the movies with friends. He doesn't have to know all of the details. I promise I'll be home by eleven and not one minute later."

Mom gave her last command, "All I can say is you better be home by eleven."

"I will be. Thanks Mom!"

I hurried through setting the table and ran to the phone to call Nancy. I was so excited. I couldn't believe it. I thought Mom only gave me permission because she wanted to meet this perfect Mr. Senior Guy who was interested in her daughter. I wasn't worried a bit. I knew Norman would impress my parents.

Norman was the perfect gentleman. He came to the door and I introduced him to Mom and he took her hand and said, "So nice to meet you Mrs. Rose." Dad was not home.

Norman opened the car door for me. It was so easy talking with him and we were laughing a lot before we even met up with his friends.

His friends climbed into the back seat and then it was continual talking. I liked his friends. I sat close to him during the movie and he held my hand. I felt so comfortable being with him and I didn't want the evening to end.

We dated for most of the school year. We had fun dates together. On cold winter days we often rode in his car with the top down and the heater on full blast. We went swimming one afternoon at the neighborhood indoor pool and even though I wasn't an avid swimmer, I had a good time. I was a terrible bowler too, but we tried our skills at the bowling alley. During spring time Norman and I laughed our way through the maze at the putt, putt miniature golf course, the sport I enjoyed the most. Late one evening we shared an innocent good-night kiss.

Then one day, Norman came over, to my house, on a motor scooter, not a motorcycle just a motor scooter. My father liked Norman, but Dad wasn't too happy that Norman drove a convertible and he really wasn't happy when he saw Norman on a motor scooter. Unfortunately, he met Norman at the driveway and told him that his daughter wasn't allowed to ride on a motor scooter. Of course when I saw Norman I begged for a ride. Norman obeyed my father's order and said no to me; but that didn't stop Norman from taking another girl for a ride.

Several days later at school Norman didn't even greet me in the hallway. He didn't look at me, let alone give his usual smile. I didn't know why and I had no idea what was wrong.

Later in the day I was in the school library with Nancy and Marilyn. I noticed they were writing notes and giggling.

"What's so funny?" I asked. I was in a rather worried mood and I didn't like hearing them laughing when I didn't know the joke.

"Oh, it's nothing." Nancy answered.

"Well," I said, "if it's nothing, why do you guys keep laughing, and what are the notes all about?"

Marilyn crumpled up the paper.

"Really," she muttered, "It's nothing - don't worry about it."

Then they started to snicker again.

"Come on you guys, what is the big secret?"

Nancy couldn't contain a secret for very long. She blurted out, "It's about Norman."

I could sense my heart beating and my eyes ready to tear. All day I had a bad feeling about why Norman was ignoring me. Now I was about to find out why and I wasn't sure I wanted to hear the reason.

"What about Norman?" I asked.

Then Marilyn turned away from me, but Nancy stated, "Norman asked Marilyn out."

I was shocked. I turned to Marilyn. "Is this true?" I asked her.

Marilyn looked right at me. "Well, kind of. He went to the church pot luck last Wednesday night with my family. So I said yes to go to the movies with him on Friday night. Besides, you guys weren't even going steady or anything like that."

True, we weren't going steady. I wasn't wearing his school ring around my neck. I didn't even know if he had a school ring. We never even talked about being a steady boy and girl friend. Even though I felt terrible, Marilyn's remarks made me believe I didn't even have a right to feel bad. Still, I felt sick. I wanted to just go somewhere and cry.

Then Nancy added one last stabbing thought, "Oh yes, Marilyn don't forget that you rode on the scooter too."

Marilyn gave her a frustrated glare! "Be quiet Nancy," she mumbled.

I figured dating Marilyn probably started out innocently. I assumed that he went to her house to visit her brother, Earl. Then he offered to take her for a ride on his motor scooter, the same scooter that my dad wouldn't allow me to ride. Then he asked her out. The part he missed was telling me he was no longer dating me.

The bell rang and I didn't want to argue anymore. I left the library by myself. I finished school that day. I fought the tears until I got home. Then I went into my bedroom lied on my bed and released my tears and sobs. I felt betrayed, not only by Norman, but also by my best friends. I had to really think about it. Marilyn and I had been friends since we were five years old. Nancy and I were friends since sixth grade. My girl friends mattered more to me than a boy friend that I had only known for a few months, even though it was a nice few months.

As the weeks went by, Marilyn and Norman continued dating. They also tried to make up for their actions by setting me up with blind dates, usually a friend of Norman's. I wrote in my diary, "Even though I want to go out, I don't want Norman to feel he has to get me a date."

They continued dating and we all remained friends. After all, that is what friendship is all about.

******

My life had been fairly easy during my childhood. I had not experienced death's sorrow, painful agony or the fear of loss until my friend Marilyn had a terrible, death-threatening accident.

69

A Tragic Day

I only heard my mother's side of the conversation. "What? There's been an accident? Was Nancy in an accident? No? Marilyn was in an accident."

Mom paused, and then continued her side of the conversation. "Oh, no. Oh, dear. That's terrible. Oh God, I am so sorry to hear this. Yes, I'll let Linda know. Please call back if there is anything we can do or if you hear more news."

Mom was trying to control her emotions. She added one last statement. "I'm just so sorry."

My mother, who seldom cried, wept out loud as she hung up the telephone. Then, as she explained to me the news, we wept together. It was February 26, 1961. Marilyn and I were fifteen years old. The phone call was from Mrs. Spencer, Nancy's mother.

There is a black and white photo of Marilyn and me dressed in sweaters and skirts standing in her back yard. It was taken, by her mother, on our first day of kindergarten. On the back of the picture is written, "1950 - Marilyn and Linda."

She was more of a "tomboy" than I was. She liked playing ball, swimming, and skiing. I liked playing with my dolls, playing house and school. I didn't play ball, I couldn't swim and my father wouldn't let me go skiing.

All we had in common was we lived close to one another and attended the same school. Marilyn would tease me. Sometimes she teased me because I mispronounced some words - I was slightly tongue-tied. There were some words I was literally unable to say correctly because my tongue did not stretch as far as it should. I doubt if Marilyn understood my predicament, though she knew I took speech therapy at school. It was a private class to teach me to stretch my tongue.

Marilyn said to the other kids, "Hey guys, come and hear Linda say aluminum. Linda say 'aluminum.'"

I would slowly repeat "aluminum," but with my teeth close together it didn't sound like aluminum. All the kids laughed.

Other times she'd go home mad because I didn't play what she wanted to play. Once, after a disagreement, I called her and her brother Earl answered the phone. He asked, "Are you calling to say you are sorry?"

I thought the argument was strictly Marilyn's fault, but because of Earl's comment, I knew that Marilyn told her family that our disagreement was entirely my fault. I soon realized that they always took her side and sometimes told Marilyn, "You shouldn't play with Linda if she isn't going to play fair."

Despite every mishap that seemed contrary to our friendship, we remained friends. Every day we played together.

This February phone call gave us the details of her accident. She had taken a ski lesson at Government Camp and was ready to leave the Timberline Lodge. At the time of the accident she and another girl, named Sally were climbing in the back of a pickup truck. Even though Marilyn's parent's owned a cabin near Mt. Hood they were trying to catch a bus back to Portland. Marilyn and Sally were going to ride in this truck for just a short distance to return to where they were to meet the bus.

When Marilyn started to climb into the bed of the truck, another nearby car "out of control" backed up. The driver did not notice that Marilyn was behind the car or wasn't able stop the car. Marilyn was pinned between the pickup truck and the car.

Her legs were crushed between the two vehicles. A doctor was there, who did what he could, but knew she needed more than he could give and an ambulance was called. The nearest hospital was

71

in Portland. The paramedic driver drove more than ninety miles per hour to save her life. Cars pulled over to let the emergency vehicle pass along the winding highway. Earl was the driver of one of those cars that veered and stopped against the roadside. He did not realize that inside the ambulance was his sister being rushed to Providence Hospital.

The news that Mom and I received, on that Sunday morning was that Marilyn had been in a terrible accident and one of her legs had been amputated.

The only time I heard about an amputation was from a scene that I had watched on television. It was a scene from World War II in which a pilot had to have his leg removed while he was still on the battle-field. It was a horrible episode where they sawed off his leg with only whiskey as an anesthetic. I cried during the film and had bad dreams and haunting memories of that scene for a long time afterwards.

I also knew the true story about a young boy who lost his leg during a train accident while he was playing on the railroad tracks. To have a leg amputated seemed like the most horrible experience of all time. I could not imagine how Marilyn could live through this tragedy.

It was several days before I was allowed to see Marilyn. Nancy and I met at Providence St. Vincent hospital near my home on 47th and Glisan. We were in the hallway when several nuns approached us and asked who we were planning to visit. When we answered, "Marilyn" they firmly told us that Marilyn was not allowed to have visitors. Marilyn overheard what they ordered. She yelled at us, "Come on in. I want to see you guys."

She expected us to walk right by these authoritative-looking nuns in their habits of stiff white nursing caps, starched white collars and long black robes. Marilyn was full of spunk even during this difficult, devastating time.

Feeling extremely intimidated, we slowly walked by the nuns and went into her room. There was Marilyn, propped up on her pillows with one leg in a cast and in traction. Her other leg, was also in traction, but only a stump way above her knee. We looked at her face and saw the same girl we knew – the bossy, controlling friend who now was going to control this crisis situation.

I feared hospitals, but Marilyn made it seem like she ran the place instead of the doctors, nurses and nuns. She politely asked for assistance when needed, but she told them what she should have, what would be best, and that her friends needed to be present.

Her second week in the hospital she celebrated her sixteenth birthday. Parents, relatives and nine classmates came into her room with cake, flowers, and balloons to party. The nuns were beside themselves. They mumbled: "This is against hospital policy. Really all of these friends should not be here at the same time. What is this girl thinking, having all these people in the room? She needs her rest!"

Marilyn was not in a resting mood. Acknowledging this special day and celebrating with her friends was her main concern. Her positive attitude prevented any of us to express sympathy for her condition. She told us that soon she would be back skiing. She had heard about a program that taught amputees how to ski. I was shocked. Several of us asked, "Really?"

Marilyn didn't know how long it would be before she could even get out of bed. She was told she would have to endure six weeks of traction, and then wear a body cast and stay in bed for five more months - all needed to save her other leg.

Finally, she was released from the hospital, but sent home in a body cast. At home she complained about being bored and she was frustrated. My dad, who always had a solution to every problem, said the way to keep Marilyn from being bored was to teach her how to play Cribbage. So he and I taught Marilyn to play Cribbage. In her bedroom Marilyn and I spent hours playing this card game.

After five long months the cast came off. She was able to be in a wheelchair. Using the wheelchair was an exciting event. It would be a while before she would be fitted for an artificial leg.

In August it was time for my family to spend a couple weeks at the beach in Seaside, Oregon. Usually, I invited friends. My mother said I should invite Marilyn to the beach. So I did. I also invited Nancy.

Nancy and I worked together to help Marilyn to do all the usual activities at the beach. The wheelchair did not do well on the sand. So we put Marilyn on a blanket and used it, like a stretcher, and carried her to the soft sand. This was complicated because the cabin we rented at the beach was near the roadside and not facing the ocean. We had to hike over a sandy knoll to reach the beach area and to see the shoreline. With Marilyn in the middle of the blanket, Nancy and I each took two corners and carried her to the sand. Near some logs we placed the blanket and Marilyn on the sand. Then we sat on the blanket too and sunbathed.

In the evenings, we pushed the wheelchair down the promenade and went to town. We wore white shorts, short- sleeve tops and matching straw hats. I think Marilyn felt accepting about herself and her condition. This was the first time she'd been out in public minus one leg. She discovered it didn't seem to matter. We flirted and the boys flirted. We jabbered and giggled like always.

Marilyn would get her replacement leg shortly after the beach trip. She would ski and swim again. She changed; she had more empathy for others. Her teasing manner was set aside for a more accepting mode.

******

In 1962 certain events occurred that would impact future decisions.

Changes

The year 1962 brought significant life changes. Within a year's time, a major national event happened that altered history. It was June. My friend Patsy had graduated from high school and I had just finished my junior year. We were getting ready to go to the Seattle World Fair: Century 21 Exposition. The fair itself would reveal predictions of the future.

We also planned to participate in visitation week at Lutheran Bible Institute. My sister paid for us to have this special week at LBI with the hope that I would like this school and I would want to attend in the fall of 1963. During this special orientation week I'd get to attend classes, meet teachers and staff members, all the while living in the dorm. Of course, I invited Patsy to join me for this summer week. I seldom went anywhere without inviting a friend to come along.

"I can't decide what to wear. What are you packing Patsy?" I walked around my bedroom, while holding the phone to my ear and dragging the long phone cord beneath my feet. I tore clothes out of my drawers and slid hangers across my closet rail. Nothing seemed perfect; my cut-off jeans were too ratty looking, my white shorts were too tight and too short, my pedal pushers looked too loose and I didn't like the pattern. I wished I had new tennis shoes. The only shoes I had, that I liked, were my sandals. I knew too that we had to take some skirts and dresses. For sure, I was taking my light pink dress. That was the one dress that I thought I looked good in.

Patsy reassured me, "Linda, don't worry about it. Just throw in some tops and shorts, a pair of jeans, a couple dresses and skirts. We can always trade clothes."

Patsy and I often traded clothes. We were close to the same size and I liked her clothes better than mine. She seemed to enjoy wearing my blouses better than hers.

"That sounds like a great idea. I feel much better now. Oh yeah, don't forget to bring me the sleeping bag you said I could borrow."

Patsy's family often went camping and they had sleeping bags. My family never went camping so usually I was borrowing a sleeping bag when I needed one.

"Let's see," I added, "what else do we need? Oh yeah, a Bible, flashlight, sunglasses, tooth brush, and swim suits, though I don't know if we will get a chance to swim or not. I'm just so excited. This is going to be so neat, Patsy. Don't you think we're going to have a great time?"

Not only did I invite friends along when I went somewhere, my sister also invited others when she had a trip planned. She and my brother-in-law Calvin were going to drive Patsy and me to Seattle. So she invited my brother Danny and our Aunt Elsie to ride along. It was like, "Let's all go to the fair!"

Susan had answered an ad in the paper and we were to stay at this home in Seattle. Many people were renting out space in their homes to accommodate all the fair goers. These people had a trailer on their property and that is where Patsy and I were to sleep that night. I was expecting a long, long trailer, but it wasn't long. It was very small; however, sleeping in tight cold, drafty quarters just added to the adventure.

Our first day at the fair was amazing. The fair opened on April 21, two months before we were there. I didn't know it then, but I read later that President Kennedy was the one who announced the opening moment of the fair. The announcement was made from a distance, since he was in Florida at the time. It was planned for him to attend the closing ceremony of the fair too, but instead he was too busy being involved with the Cuban Missile Crisis. At the time the public thought that the reason he did not attend was because he was sick with a common cold, an excuse that everyone could relate to and would understand.

This Saturday morning the weather was rather gray and foggy. Calvin had to pay for parking, but at last we were at the fairgrounds.

There were flags everywhere depicting various countries. Most people were wearing coats because the morning air was breezy. There were also many people from other countries wearing their traditional attire. "People watching" was fun. I also enjoyed staring at the various fountains spraying water in different directions.

What I wanted to see the most was the Space Needle that was built especially for this event. I had heard about it, but the advertised details did not describe what I saw. It was unbelievable. Here was a tower sixty stories tall. I had never seen such a high building. It was shaped like a spaceship and on top was a revolving restaurant called, "Eye of the Needle." I could not imagine a restaurant that moved. Of course, it rotated very slowly. If you sat, ate and stayed for an hour, your view out the window would change. Amazing!

By three in the afternoon Patsy and I had left the family to explore the fair on our own. The sun was now bright and the sky was clear. "Are you scared?," I asked Patsy as we stood waiting for our turn to ride up the elevator to the observation deck of the Space Needle.

I had never seen an elevator with glass walls surrounding the sides. Actually, I enjoyed elevator rides and thought it would be fun to be an elevator operator. But this was different from any store elevator I had been in before.

Patsy was always eager to try daring and new experiences. "No," she said, "I'm not scared. It will be fun!"

"Do you realize that we will be riding up this elevator and within forty-three seconds we will be at the top? I feel like I'm waiting for a roller coaster ride rather than an elevator ride."

"Linda," Patsy sighed, "you worry too much."

Actually, when we got into the elevator, it was Patsy who closed her eyes and wouldn't even look at the ground beneath us. I enjoyed every second.

From the painted bright orange observation deck, we viewed the colorful fairground tents below. We were up 650 feet and higher than any other structure in Seattle. The town streets appeared miniature with small cars and buses moving across the way. Looking to the distance, we saw Mount Rainier, the water view of Puget Sound and the white snowy Olympic and Cascade Mountains. I didn't mind leaning out over the closest steel rail to see as much as I was able to see and to feel the cool breeze. Besides having a close rail to grip my hands on to, there was the security of the other iron rails surrounding the entire circular deck. I realized then that this Space Needle was going to be a lasting landmark for Seattle. I was thrilled that I was one of the first million people to experience the excitement of this new structure.

Everything at the fair was amazing. The "World of the Future" demonstrated air cars that would run on electrically- controlled highways. We watched as a lady from Bell Telephone demonstrated the latest phone inventions: call waiting, push button (instead of rotary dialing systems) and an example of a phone that would actually let you not only hear, but also see the person on the other line. I was very concerned about this concept. I spent a lot of time during my teen years talking on the phone. Most of these times I didn't want the person on the other end of the line to know what I was doing or what I looked like at the moment, so I wasn't too thrilled about this future possibility. I feared that it would happen too soon for my liking.

That evening we attended the Tommy Bartlett Water Show. This was a group of water skiers who did their tricks in a million-gallon circular water tank in a large stadium. The boat sped around in the tank and the skiers jumped over the waves and then stacked themselves into a pyramid formation.

The next day Calvin drove us to Lutheran Bible Institute in North Seattle. There my sister and family said their goodbyes. The very first moment I saw the campus I felt at home. The main building was large, tan and framed with bricks. The building sat off the main road and was surrounded by grass and trees. It included the fellowship hall, front office, dining room, chapel area, women's dormitory rooms, a studio apartment (where the dean of women stayed), a basement with ping pong tables and laundry facilities. Directly across the main office was a sunken living room that had a home- like atmosphere. On one wall there were four plate glass windows that went from floor to ceiling. On the back wall was a red brick, wood burning fireplace. The floor was wooden with one large circular plaid rag rug in the center. The room's furniture - couches, chairs, end tables, lamps and even a piano in one corner; made for a comfortable setting. What was absent was a television set. There was no TV or radio in this gathering room, but that would change. It would be months away, but there would come a time when the national news would necessitate adding a television.

There was another long narrow newer building which included classrooms. It had a slanted roof with high windows. Further down the campus was a separate house where the boys' dorm was located.

Our temporary dorm rooms were upstairs in the main building. The restrooms and showers were down the hallway. Our room had two beds, two desks, two large closets, and a sink and a mirror area. On the outside wall was a large window. Even though it was rather bare, without bedding or extra personal touches, it was warm and inviting. This was the room that Patsy and I were to share for the week.

"Come Patsy, let's tour the campus." We plopped our sleeping bags and luggage on the separate twin beds and headed out the doorway. We were only two doors down the hallway when I started screaming, "Karen, Paula! I can't believe you guys are here. This is just so way cool! Patsy, this is Karen and this is Paula." I introduced her to special friends I knew from Camp Colton.

Immediately, I felt like I belonged at this school. Classes hadn't even started and I already knew two girls that I and my other friend Nancy had been very close with during our summer camp week.

Karen and Paula gave Patsy and me each a warm, welcoming hug. These Christian friends always greeted each other with hugs. Patsy was somewhat reserved, but she joined in and the four of us linked our arms together. Then, like Dorothy going down the yellow brick

79

road, we skipped down the wide hallway. We were heading out the doorway to see and to greet others at LBI.

That evening the whole student body gathered together in the fellowship hall. The school director, Pastor Stime, enthusiastically welcomed us by introducing himself with a taunting invitation, "I challenge you to demonstrate to us whatever talent you have." Then he demonstrated his talent by standing on his head. Of course all of us were shocked. He said he could stand on his head longer than any one of us and during the week he offered to prove this to be true if anyone challenged his statement. Students came forward to show their specific talent. Some whistled, some did cartwheels and flips; one gal was able to stretch her leg straight up over her head. I decided that the only gift I might have that would compete with these examples was the ability to bend back my thumb to touch my arm, which I did proceed to do in front of everyone. This was one way that the LBI staff helped us to feel accepted and welcomed.

During the forthcoming week, I made some self-discoveries. I decided that I liked taking showers. Usually, at home, I only took baths. I also decided that studying isn't bad when you like the subject that you are studying (I really enjoyed studying the Bible). I experienced a new bonding with fellow teens and realized how exciting it was to talk to other students about God, the Bible, religion, daily living and temptation. There was a sense of common fellowship when we prayed together. I also surprised myself - I was good at playing ping pong!

In the middle of the week a bus took all of us to the fair. This fair day included a short but awesome ride on the monorail. We also went to the water show one more time. Another day was spent at the beach swimming and enjoying the sun until I was sunburned. During chapel time we saw slides from the Bible lands of Egypt and listened to a missionary from Germany. Patsy and I spent a long time visiting with Ezra, another student, a young black man from Ethiopia. One afternoon Patsy and I played pianos - there were two pianos in one of the large rooms and we entertained ourselves. The last day we cried during the inspirational chapel service.

At the end of the week Patsy's parents came up to take us home. I still had another year of high school to complete. I made it my goal to do well my senior year because my plan was to come back to LBI where I already felt at home.

After my high school graduation, in the fall of 1963, I enrolled at LBI as a full time student. On November 22, 1963, the school staff decided that it was vital that a television set be placed in the lobby reception room. They knew about the CBS News bulletin from Dallas, Texas.

"Three shots have been fired at President Kennedy." History was happening live on television. We all became witnesses to the horrific event.

On black and white television we heard the snapping sound of the shots and saw our president fall backward from his seated position in the convertible open car, witnessed the parade crowd running wildly and diving to the ground for protection. We heard the sirens echoing in the background. In agony we waited, as did the rest of the world, to hear if our president was still alive.

We were students who were living under government leadership that citizens were calling "Camelot." We really trusted our president. We felt comfortable with our world, but on November 22 we saw on television, our leader get assassinated. We prayed and held onto the hope of our president living. Then we heard the devastating message, repeated several times: "With the greatest regret President Kennedy is dead. The Associated Press just reported two priests have declared President Kennedy is dead."

Though we mourned, there was a sense of unity and comfort because we shared this experience as Christian believers. It was meaningful when together we sang:

"Eternal Father, strong to save, Whose arm has bound the restless wave, Who bade the mighty ocean deep its own appointed limits keep: O hear us when we cry to Thee For those in peril on the sea."

President Kennedy once saved men at sea; we felt like we were lost in a sea of sadness and a nation without its earthly leader.

Every day, for hours, we watched the television reports. We were too stunned to think clearly, too emotional to cry alone, and too tense to leave the news reports. The drama was still happening. The accused sole assassin, Lee Harvey Oswald, was arrested after he shot a police officer. Then, on November 24 we witnessed, on live television, the assassin getting shot. Just as they were transferring Oswald from the county courthouse to the jail a man, later identified as Jack Ruby, shot him. The news was happening right before our eyes. There was a sense that events were out of anyone's control.

We shared our lingering grief on November 25 while the world viewed the royal funeral of our leader; we became more united as we lived through these historic events together.

I will always remember where I was during the years of 1962 and 1963. I vividly remember the day of November 22, 1963. I am thankful that I was at LBI with others who believed in eternal life and expressed hope for the future, despite the tragedy of the day.

******

When my family went on our family vacation in 1962, Marilyn had a wooden leg and was able to walk and drive. She drove herself and our friend Nancy to join us in Seaside.

82

The Riot

When I was young our vacation times were at Seaside, Oregon. Seaside is a beach town with the main street headed toward sand and the Pacific Ocean. For two weeks every summer we vacationed at the same cabins. They were on the north side of Seaside owned by the York family. They were called the York cabins.

The north side of Seaside isn't the crowded town side. The cabins we stayed in were several blocks from the end of the promenade. Often we walked on the prom, over a mile, to the town center.

Our end of the beach seemed like our private territory, with few people. These cottages did not face the shoreline. We had to climb over a sand dune to see the vast ocean. In front of the sand hillside, was a gravel road with briar stickers that clung to our feet. I often walked to the beach with bare feet. Then I would have to pull these small thorns out from the flat part of my foot. Sometimes I was smart enough to wear sandal thongs. On the beach I went barefoot and enjoyed sliding my feet across the soft, smooth, warm sand.

My dad came to the beach only on the weekends. Then he'd go back home to his work schedule. My mother would be there the whole two weeks. My younger brother, Danny and my older sister, Susan, came too. Sometimes my aunt and cousins came to the beach. They would be there because my uncles fished in Astoria. Many times I'd bring my friends along.

If relatives came they would rent their own cabins in the same courtyard. These rentals were not luxury units; rather, they were small, clean and comfortable. We didn't have a television. Our cabin entertainment depended on reading Bible stories, playing games, and enjoying meal time socials. While basking at the beach we'd have long conversations. At night we talked until the wee hours.

At the seashore my friends and I splashed in the ocean, walked the length of the shoreline, and bathed in the sun.

Late in the afternoon we sometimes hiked into town.

A couple times we even rented bikes and explored the surrounding area.

On August 19, 1962 my family went to the beach. I was sixteen years old and my dad actually let me drive the ninety miles from Portland to Seaside. As soon as we reached the beach Danny and I headed for the ocean. Amazingly the cold Pacific water felt rather warm. I often sensed the ocean calling me. Then I had to run into the waves and feel the white foam licking my skin. This was one of those calling days.

Late that afternoon, my dad left to return home. That evening my mom, Danny and I went on a long walk. I was anxious for the next day to come because my friends would be coming to the beach.

Nancy, Marilyn and I were all in the same grade at school. I was the youngest by several months. They were seventeen and I was sixteen. Even though we were three young teenage girls, there was no fear of us having too much freedom at the beach. We felt perfectly safe at Seaside. I think my parents were not too worried about us running around together. There was this belief that we were "good girls" and certainly not out looking for trouble.

Marilyn had recently got her driver's license, and the use of her dad's car, so she drove herself and Nancy to Seaside. Using her artificial leg, she was doing quite well walking and getting around. She had a positive, "get up and go" attitude. Mostly, her disability didn't seem like a disability.

I was very happy and giddy with excitement when Marilyn drove the car into the driveway the next morning. We had no idea that later in the week there would be an event that would change the atmosphere of the peaceful town of Seaside.

"Well, it's about time you guys got here? What took you so long?" I was glad to see them. I had been extremely anxious waiting for their arrival.

Marilyn was quick to give an explanation for being late, "You know Nancy, it took her forever to get packed, and of course she brought way too much."

Nancy was quick to respond, "I did not. I just brought what I need."

"You need two suitcases?" Marilyn just rolled her eyes. I grabbed Marilyn's one duffle bag while Nancy took both of her suitcases. Then I yelled at Danny to come and help us unpack the car.

"Oh, by the way, Dad sent us some breakfast rolls." Marilyn's father was a baker and anything he sent was definitely going to be delicious.

"Oh yeah," added Marilyn "another reason we were late is Nancy couldn't decide if she should really come or not."

"Why not?" I looked at Nancy for the answer.

"Well, I got a call from Donny's mother last night. Donny is coming home in two days." Donny had been Nancy's on and off boyfriend for the last year. He was in the Air Force and stationed in Texas.

I thought about how wonderful it would be to have a steady boyfriend wanting to see me. "Wow, maybe you should have stayed home and greeted him."

"No, I really wanted to come here." Then she paused. "I don't know what I really want. But I'm here now, so if Donny wants to see me, I guess he'll just have to wait."

I felt a little worried about her decision. Donny was really a nice guy that Nancy talked about a lot and I thought if she didn't take time to greet him that their friendship might not continue. I didn't share my feelings though because mostly I wanted to spend time with my friends and not worry about any decisions.

85

We spent the rest of the afternoon on the beach. Our problem was the wind and the sand blowing in our faces. Once Marilyn got settled on the beach, we didn't move a lot because it was hard for her to maneuver on the soft sand. So we stayed by one log, but kept changing positions trying to avoid the sand blowing in our eyes. On this particular windy day it seemed hopeless. As I stood and brushed the sand off myself I said, "I have an idea. Tomorrow let's buy a wind breaker to block the wind and keep this sand from blowing in our faces."

The next day purchasing a wind breaker became our primary goal. Marilyn drove us into town. We went to one of the main variety stores. Marilyn and I quickly selected the "perfect" wind breaker. It was blue and had white canvas strips. It was on a wooden frame and could be folded for storage. It provided a good three feet of wind gust protection.

"I like this one better. It is red, white and blue." Nancy had wandered off to the other side of the store where there were more expensive wind breakers.

Marilyn and I had already agreed. We liked the blue and white one. It was the best. We knew that we would have to pool our money to make the purchase.

"Okay," Marilyn began explaining our plan, "we'll buy this blue and white one, each of us will pay $1.50, it will be used at the beach and then we'll take turns storing it at our houses till our next beach trip. This will be joint ownership. Agreed?"

Nancy and I seldom argued with Marilyn. We just dug into our pockets and handed our dollars and coins to Marilyn. Marilyn paid the total cost of $4.50. We made our first threesome big purchase, which pretty much meant that we had a lifetime commitment of being together, if for no other reason than to share this wind breaker.

The rest of the day we wandered around town. The town was crowded. We met some guys who called themselves "The Four Gems." They were a musical group playing at one of the hotels.

Nancy always had a natural talent for attracting male interest. Once we got the guys attention, Marilyn and I were quite capable of continuing the conversations. No sooner had the Four Gems gone their way, when a couple cute guys riding on motor scooters stopped to talk to us. They went with us to the Penney Arcade where we spent time trying to outdo the games. They actually treated us by paying for the games. Then we all went for a Ferris Wheel ride.

During the late afternoon, we met some guys that were stationed at Camp Rilea with the National Guard. They were in town just having fun. We didn't know it then, but before the week was out they would be ordered to be in town on duty. By the time we got back to the cabins, we felt like we had experienced a successful day.

It was just the beginning of meeting boys. We met Carl who also was staying in the York cabins with his family. He was seventeen too, and good looking. My mom took all of us horse backing riding and Carl went with us. Carl stayed up late visiting with us. Our conversations were lively and full of laughter. Marilyn, Nancy and I liked Carl.

We spent time lying on the beach, enjoying our new wind-breaker, jumping the waves in the ocean, and swimming a couple times in town at the pool. During our late evenings we spent time playing board games and talking.

On our last night at the beach - September 1 - our fun, exciting vacation resulted in a fearful evening. Carl and his family had already left town, headed back to Portland. Of course, we all gave Carl our phone numbers. Each one of us hoped he would call. Nancy had left the previous day, taking the bus back to Portland. She had decided to cut her vacation time, and go back to see Donny.

Marilyn and I were on our own. Marilyn drove and we went back to downtown Seaside where we parked the car a few blocks from the main street. The town was full of young kids (some high school teenagers, and a lot of college students). Groups of boys and girls, dressed in swim suits or shorts, were playing football and volley ball on the sand. Beach fires were burning and kites were flying. There were also a lot of beer parties on the beach.

Guys yelled at us to come join their groups. A couple good-looking guys with tan, shirtless bodies and jean shorts came up to the prom and directly approached us. They each held a beer can. "Hey, pretty girls, come on down to the beach. We've got plenty of booze and a nice fire going."

My friends and I always had a firm agreement that we would not mingle with guys that were drinking beer. Marilyn was a Mormon and her religion was against drinking. I was a Lutheran; all I knew about drinking was having a sip of communion wine. We really didn't discuss it much, but we did have this common understanding that we were not into drinking.

Marilyn was quick to give a no. "Thanks guys, but we're doing fine."

The boys continued the conversation, "Where are you from?"

I was smiling and enjoying the attention. "We're from Portland. We go to Grant High." (I really went to Washington High, but it was simpler to just mention one well-known school.) "Where are you guys from?"

"Hey, we're from Portland too. We're students at Portland State." The fact that they were in college and we were still in high school, and it didn't bother them, was another plus.

"Come on over to our fire and we'll get better acquainted."

The invitation was very tempting. They were so good looking. The tallest guy tried a different approach.

"I know," he joked, "They need a formal invitation. We cordially invite you to join our beach party."

His friend picked up the idea. "We request the honor of your presence." Then they chanted back and forth.

"We implore you to join us."

"We humbly beseech your attendance."

"If we had the means to do so, we would send you an engraved invitation; however, under the circumstances, why not just take a chance and join us?"

I enjoyed their sense of humor. The whole situation got more and more tempting.

Marilyn stood firm. We both laughed, but she stated, "It's been great talking to you guys, but we're not joining you on the beach. Have fun. Maybe, we'll see you later. Bye."

We continued walking and that was the end of that tempting invitation. We stayed on the turnaround area watching the cars cruise round and round the Lewis and Clark statue, at the end of the main street overlooking the beach. We were having fun being part of the young crowd scene.

It wasn't until around 6:00 p.m. when the happy, carefree scene started to change. The crowd got rowdier, louder and more demanding. Now when guys started to yell at us they did not easily accept our no's. They started to push closer toward us. Beer bottles were thrown and cars were honking. The noise became louder. It no longer sounded like innocent fun, or a giddy party, instead, guys were yelling and swearing at one another. It seemed like we were quiet onlookers, and were in the minority. The majority of kids were drinking and now demonstrating their rebellious side. These mass of kids become one large mob.

The police showed their presence, and they walked the streets and mingled with the crowds. By 8:30 p.m. officers questioned some kids. There was tension in the air that wasn't there earlier in the day.

By 9:00 p.m. some kids got arrested for throwing beer bottles, and for being drunk and disorderly. A group of them ran through the streets, not respecting store front properties or bystanders. Other guys got more extreme and tried to pull down the lifeguard tower on the beach.

I was nervous. I made a decision and I yelled at Marilyn, so she could hear me over the crowd noise, "I think we better leave."

I knew that Marilyn was unable to run if we needed to escape. I didn't know if I could protect her if we really got into a situation where we might be surrounded by unruly guys that wouldn't let us by or tried to harm us.

Marilyn was curious and seemed to like watching the excitement. She wasn't as scared as I was feeling. She said, "Oh, I've been through worse than this. Let's just stay till ten. Your mom said we didn't have to be back at the cabin till ten. We might as well hang out till then."

I think Marilyn felt that since she had spent weeks in the hospital and months in a body cast, being in this situation was nothing compared to what she had previously faced. As the crowd got larger, more aggressive and at times pushing against us as we moved down the sidewalk, Marilyn finally agreed that we should leave. We left the main street and headed toward the car. As soon as we turned the corner, there were fewer people and a greater sense of safety.

In some ways I felt disappointed that we left the exciting action. I knew already that what we were experiencing would probably be a news report in the morning. A crowd mob became a monster. People were following the crowd as if they were not thinking about consequences. The number of youth, onlookers and drunks were taking over the town. The police were few in number and it looked as if they were not able to control the situation. No longer was it the safe family sea side town that was so familiar. Instead, it became a scary place. I knew we had to leave.

We made it back safely to the cabins. The next day, as we left town, we bought a Seaside Signal newspaper. On the front page was the headline, "Seaside Riot, National Guard Called to Assist." I remember the guys we met earlier and spent time with - I figured they had to come back into town in uniform and armed to help control the riot. I just wanted to think about the fun time we had earlier not about the youth that were destroying the town and the peaceful atmosphere.

When we arrived back home, in Portland, I wrote in my diary, "The day of September 1, 1962 Read All About It...."

******

Soon we would be a part of another news event.

The Storm

Common sense told us we should go straight home, but our youthful daring spirits whispered, "Keep going." We thought the storm wasn't too bad. We figured the wind would probably quiet down shortly. Never before had we experienced such a storm. For us it was more exciting than fearful.

We were in Marilyn's parents' 1957 Ford Station Wagon and she was driving. It had been over a year since her bad accident. Now she was comfortable with her artificial leg. She used only her right leg and foot for the gas and brake pedal; she had no problem operating the vehicle. Matter-of-fact, out of the three of us she was the most experienced driver. Once she got her driver's license she drove to school everyday. Driving was more common for her than for Nancy and me. Nancy, who lived with her mom only, was allowed to drive when her mom wasn't using the car, and my chances to drive happened when my dad gave me permission to use his car. Marilyn's dad also had a delivery truck and her mother didn't drive so Marilyn used the car often.

This afternoon, we had met after school to go shopping. Our goal was to go to the open shopping mall, Lloyd Center in NE Portland. We didn't have a lot of money, but we each had a goal and we usually completed our goals, at least our fun ones. I wanted to buy a pair of shoes, Marilyn wanted to apply for a job at Lerners, and Nancy just liked shopping in general.

They left Grant High School and came to my house. I was living on SE Stark Street. It was a typical, windy fall day. It was Columbus Day, October 12, 1962. It was 4:00 p.m. The KISN radio station music was blaring. Bill Haley and the Comets were singing "Rock Around the Clock." As we headed to Lloyd Center Marilyn and I were singing the words, and swaying to the music.

Marilyn stopped her swaying because she became more conscious of her driving. We noticed several traffic signals that were not working. She decided to go down a side street to avoid the intersections that didn't have working lights. We drove on 28th Street; the trees were swaying, and branches were breaking. We saw one big branch fall just a few feet in front of our car with a loud thud.

"Maybe, driving down these side streets isn't such a good idea," I tried to casually suggest to Marilyn. Telling Marilyn what to do didn't always work. This time Nancy agreed with me.

"Yeah, Marilyn," Nancy warned, "there are too many trees here. Let's head back to 33rd Street."

Marilyn agreed with us. She maneuvered the car around the branches and headed for 33rd Street. Marilyn was use to obstacles in her young life. She acted like this wind storm was a minor concern.

The song ended and the radio announcer just made one simple comment, "Rather windy outside, and we've got word some traffic signals are out, so beware folks, now here's Elvis singing, "Peace in the Valley."

It was rather an odd song to be hearing during the mist of the storm, but we didn't feel it was a warning; we just continued our drive to Lloyd Center.

Marilyn parked her car in one of the upper lots. Several people were quickly leaving Lloyd Center. We felt the gusts of wind push against our bodies as we got out of the car. Marilyn was not that firm on her feet so I stood on one side and Nancy stood on the other. With the wind pressing at our backs, our hair blowing in disarray, and our jackets flapping we slowly walked to the first nearby building. We got inside and discovered that we were at Newberry's lunch counter.

We felt so successful that we made it inside safely that we decided to stay and sit at the counter, and eat something.

The waiter came over and told us we could not sit by the counter because one of the glass plate windows had already blown out. He suggested we sit in one of the side booths. Then we noticed the piece of plywood over the place where the glass had shattered. Wow, this storm was worse than we thought.

We didn't want to leave the view of the window where we could see the trees swaying and debris blowing down the street; however, we did as we were told and went over to the booth area. I thought I was hungry, but I was also nervous. Instead of ordering my usual hamburger and milk shake I decided just to get a chocolate milk shake. I thought we should hurry and get our errands done and get home before dark. Then I remembered that home for me was across town and home for Marilyn and Nancy was closer. Maybe having Marilyn drive me all the way home in the storm was not a good idea.

The restaurant was not quiet; we could hear the sound of the wind howling so loud it sounded like continuous thunder. The few customers who were there talked only about the storm.

"Isn't this rather unusual for Portland?"

"Yes, it is especially around this time of year."

"Well, it's bound to let up soon so I'm just going to wait it out."

"I wonder how fast this wind is blowing."

"Please folks, don't get near the plate glass window."

The comments continued all the time we were eating. We didn't know what the latest news was about the storm. There wasn't a radio or television set in the restaurant.

As the storm continued, and we drank our milk shakes (all three of us decided on milk shakes only), we concluded that we had better skip our shopping goals and head for home.

Once again, we went out to fight the gusts of wind. I mentioned that I would bring the car to Marilyn rather than her struggling across the parking lot again. Marilyn was stubborn. "No," she said, "I can make it. The wind can't be that bad."

So once again Nancy stood close to her on one side and I stood on the other side. The sky was somewhat bright, but with numerous clouds moving quickly. The air seemed heavy like there was pressure pressing against us. I was breathing a smell like a normal damp, fall day, but without the crisp clean whiff of air, rather a heavy breath of smog.

When I was a small child, I actually feared the wind because my brother-in-law teased me saying that I was so thin I would just blow away. This time though, I wasn't fearful for myself; I was more aware of protecting Marilyn from falling than I was about my ability to stand firm.

We trudged back to the car successfully. We looked at the littered parking lot. Papers, leaves, tree branches, were making a mess of the pavement. We agreed going to my house was out of the question and that we would just head to Nancy's apartment; then Marilyn could get the car home because that was only another two blocks.

We turned on the radio. This time they were not playing music. The announcer was focused on giving detailed storm information: "We have a special announcement. The winds have picked up to forty miles per hour. A safety alert has been posted. People are asked to stay off the streets. Stay home until the storm subsides."

Oops, we missed obeying that safety tip. We were in the midst of the mess and now we had to keep heading home. If we didn't get home soon we knew our parents would be upset. Marilyn was concerned now, not so much for our safety, but if a tree limb fell on the car she knew she'd be in trouble.

Marilyn drove way below the speed limit. We traveled about 20 miles an hour on streets that we usually drove between 35 and 40 miles per an hour. We felt the car shake with the force of the wind. The wind sounds didn't subside even for a few minutes - it was a constant sound like a hissing sound with a slight whistle.

I was seated in the front seat and Nancy was in the back. Marilyn ordered us to be "extra eyes" and to watch for flying branches or even falling trees. So we yelled out orders and warnings. "Steer to the right. There are too many trees on the left side of the road."

"I think it would be better if we just drove more in the middle of the road."

"Watch it! What is that black streak across the road up ahead? Could it be a power line?"

"I don't think we should even go that way to find out. Let's just go around the corner here and up Klickitat Street." I was forgetting that Klickitat Street was full of trees. It seemed that every street was lined with more trees than usual.

Marilyn turned at the corner and started up the side road. We heard rocks, bits of metal, acorns, chestnuts, and swags from trees tapping on the side of the car. It was as if we were being hit by debris even if we were not running over debris.

We continued to slowly inch our way forward. Normally, these three miles would be such a short distance. It seemed like we were going a long ways just to get to Nancy's apartment. Of course, we had never driven this slowly before.

After many fearful moments, we finally got to our last main intersection. It was the corner of Fremont. A cream colored Chevy was off to the side of the road with a heavy, huge tree limb resting on its top. The police were there. We really couldn't tell if someone was still in the car or not, but it did not look good. The signals did not work so Marilyn did not stop for long, just long enough to let another car pass. Now we only had a few blocks to go.

Finally, we made it to Nancy's. We giggled with relief. "Wow, what an experience," Nancy sighed.

I opened the car door and could barely stand up against the wind, "I can't believe this wind. I don't think I can shut the door."

Nancy helped by pushing the car door closed. We were still laughing as we thanked Marilyn. Our uncontrollable laughter did not help to control our bodies that were being pushed by wind gusts. We yelled at Marilyn that we would call her dad and let him know she would be home in a couple minutes.

We staggered up Nancy's stairs to her apartment door as if we had been drinking wine instead of milk shakes. We knew Nancy's mother was not home. She was at Poncho's Restaurant working.

When we got inside the apartment we discovered there was no power; however, her phone did work. We called Marilyn's dad so he would know that Marilyn was on her way and he'd have the garage door open for her.

Other than not having power, Nancy's place seemed fine. It was protected from the wind by the surrounding apartments. It was rather quiet inside compared to the noise we had been experiencing out in the middle of the storm.

We were only there for a few minutes when my dad came knocking on the door. He had been all the way out to Beaverton to pick up my mom from work. In the car were Mom and my brother. He only came over to check on me. Once he saw that I was fine he suggested I stay with Nancy since she was all alone. He said that he was headed home and he would call us when he got there. He kissed me on the cheek good-bye. At the time, I didn't think about how worried I would be having my family back out in the storm.

Nancy and I looked for candles. We tried to figure out what to do in her semi-dark apartment.

Her phone still worked so, after an hour I repeatedly called home. I let the phone ring over and over. I counted the rings: ten, eleven, twelve. Then I would hang up and confront Nancy, as if it was her fault, "Why aren't they answering the phone?"

Nancy reassured me by saying, "They probably aren't there yet. Remember we had to drive really slowly I'm sure your parents are taking it slow too."

"Yeah," I responded in exasperation "but it shouldn't take over an hour to get across town."

Finally, Mrs. Spencer, Nancy's mom, came home. She was glad to see that we were safe. She had her own story about trying to stay at work until the restaurant had to close because they lost their power. Then she told about how hard it was to drive from Sandy Boulevard to the apartment. She suggested we go in the garage and listen to the car radio reports to see what was happening around town.

On some stations we only heard static air and then we heard these announcements: "The winds have peaked up to 116 miles an hour. Residents are asked to stay inside their homes and seek shelter. Do not go out into the streets. Power lines are down, several trees down near SE Stark Street. It is very dangerous to be out on the roads tonight. We already have reported injuries and deaths. We have word that this storm is affecting all of Oregon and Washington. It is said to be from a storm out in the Pacific Ocean, named Typhoon Freda. Folks, we are now experiencing a hurricane category-three storm. We repeat, do not go out into the streets tonight." Portland Public Schools have already announced there will be no school on Monday. Governor Mark Hatfield will be calling for National Guardsman for cleanup storm aid. This is KGW am 620 radio - stay tuned for further weather related reports."

Stark Street was where my family lived. Our house was on 35th and Stark. I was even more concerned now. I also felt like I should have been with my family because they were experiencing all this excitement and I wasn't part of it.

They were in the middle of a news-breaking disaster while I sat safely in Nancy's garage only hearing about what was happening.

Once we got back to the apartment, I called home again. I couldn't believe that my dad would forget to call me. The phone was ringing. I visualized my parents' house empty, dark and a phone ringing over and over.

Finally, around 9:00 p.m. the wind hushed. It was like nothing had happened. It was too dark to see what damage was done.

I called my folks again - still no answer. Around 11:00 we went to bed. I did not go to sleep; I was concerned about my family. Why didn't they call me?

Early the next morning the phone rang. Mrs. Spencer answered the phone. "Hello? Oh, hi Marilyn. Yeah, the girls are up and we are eating some cold cereal. Sure enough, our power is still out, but I do have a gas stove and an ice box where I'm keeping the milk cold. How about your family? No power, but everyone is safe? Well good. Well, I reckon they can."

She held the phone in one hand and turned to us, "Would y'all like to go ride out to the city dump with Marilyn, Norm and Earl?"

Mrs. Spencer said the boys had been clearing tree limbs from Marilyn's folks' driveway all morning and they had a trailer full and Mr. Landsborough, Marilyn's dad, wanted it dumped "Now."

I was thrilled to get out and see what damage the storm had caused. "Sure," I said, "but can they take me home afterwards?"

Mrs. Spencer asked Marilyn if that would work and Marilyn said, "Fine."

We rode in the Ford station wagon that was pulling a trailer full of debris. It was then we noticed the devastation from the night before. Every street was full of branches, garbage and limbs. It was as if a giant had stomped through the town during the night and destroyed everything he touched, including sweeping away roof shingles as he passed by.

Even though it was only around ten in the morning, the dump was a busy place. Cars were lined up. Every car had a trailer of tree limbs and shingle pieces and metal scraps to throw away.

It took us a long, slow time to get across town, but finally we made it to my house. The first thing I noticed was our huge fir tree, which I liked to look up at and see the blue sky above, was now only a half tree. It had been split right down the middle. My parents' car was in the driveway so I figured they really did make it home. I said a quick good-by to my friends and I ran up the front porch cement steps. I opened the front door. There was Dad sitting in the living room reading the paper. Mom was working in the kitchen with her apron hanging over her dress.

"Well, you're home." My dad didn't bother getting up, but just gave me a quick glance.

"Yeah, I'm home" I said. "Why didn't you guys call me last night?"

"We couldn't call you. The phone is dead." Mom came out of the kitchen and agreed, "Yes, Linda, the phone is dead."

"I went over to the hall stand and picked up the black rotary phone. Instead of the dial tone all I heard was silence."

"Well," I defensively yelled, "you should have figured out some way to call me at Nancy's." Tears came to my eyes. "The point is, Dad, you always worry about me, but do you ever think I might worry about you guys?" Then, with a crying voice, I continued, "I spent all night worrying why you didn't call."

"Well, I don't see what all the fuss is about. We're all fine. So no point worrying."

That was Dad. He seldom understood why someone else would worry or be upset.

The storm was over. The power was off. I thought about taking a shower, but instead I went to my room and flopped on my bed. I wiped the tears off my cheek; I wrote in my diary, "Oct. 12, no electricity, no TV, no radio, no phone and no hot water."

******

Nancy and I did the usual teenage activities, but we also sought for spiritual growth. Often we discussed questions about God and what we believed. To answer some of our wondering thoughts we visited other churches especially during their evening services.

New Church Experiences

During our senior year in high school Nancy and I decided to visit a variety of church services. On Sunday evenings we attended different churches than the traditional ones that we worshiped in every Sunday morning. Nancy was a Baptist; I was a Lutheran. I had attended the same church since I was a baby, St. Paul Lutheran Church, though it wasn't the same church building. At first the church was at 12th and Clinton in Portland. Now a newer church building was located at 3880 SE Brooklyn Street.

We liked our traditions and our morning worship services, but we wanted to see what the other churches offered too. One of our evening churches was an Evangelical Free church that had lots of gospel singing at their evening service and it was a lively program. Then we found a church that was even more awake than the Evangelical church. We discovered a church in North East Portland the Metropolitan Church of God. Most of the parishioners were black people and the services were filled with spontaneous amens and singing expressions that the black people can freely do.

One of the Pastor's sermons that penetrated my mind was the story of the Prodigal son from Luke 15. The year I heard this sermon from Pastor Wendell Wallace I bought a book of his sermons titled, "Giving the Pigs a Permanent Wave." I still have this book, written in 1963. Pastor Wallace's summary of the seven lessons from this story are: "You are only young once, there is no place like home, all that Glitters is not gold, you never miss the water until the well goes dry, a good run is better than a bad stand, a stitch in time saves nine and the greatest thing in the world is love."

Nancy and I sat in the pews listening to Pastor Wallace as he held the Bible in his left hand and used gestures to emphasize his points with his right hand. I remember his excitement of telling the story straight and true and with power as congregational members encouraged him with their shouts of "Amen" and "you tell them brother. Hallelujah."

"Young people, O young people, before you go too far, Stop! Turn around before it's too late. You may think you don't need the Church, the Bible, or Jesus Christ, but there is a day coming when your well of dissipation is going to run dry. You will hunger for those times of fellowship with God's people. Memory will haunt you of the 'good ole days' you had with the saints of God. Look at the Prodigal as he reminisces in the hog pen. The Holy Spirit is bringing to His remembrance the 'good things promised to those who walk uprightly.' Can't you remember those times? Now where are your 'fair-weathered' friends? Ninety nine out of every one hundred friends that the devil introduces to you will desert you when the shrieking winds begin to howl. But wait a minute! The Prodigal Son is coming to himself...listen: 'How many hired servants of my father's have bread and enough to spare, and I perish with hunger! I will arise and go to my father.' At last he is getting some sense. He has found out that A Good Run is Better than a Bad Stand."

With preaching like that there was no chance of day dreaming or not paying attention to the sermon. It was exciting! Nancy and I went back often on Sunday evenings to hear Pastor Wallace give us the inspiration to remain strong in our faith during our teen years.

******

During my senior year of high school a counselor told me I wasn't "college material." I figured my goals were not achievable, but a transformation happened that made college possible.

PART III

OUR
COLLEGE
YEARS

College Days

While in high school studying was almost impossible for me. I was busy with family activities and more concerned with what my friends were doing than finishing school assignments. Also, I was stubborn. One time, in my drama class, I had read a play and wrote a summary about that play, and turned in the paper. Then the drama teacher insisted that I read a different book and write another report to satisfy the requirements. I refused. I told the teacher, "I already read a play. I already wrote the assignment, I don't see any need to rewrite it."

My school friends begged me to just do the paper rather than get a low grade. I stuck to what I thought was right and fair. I did not redo the assignment. I got a D.

When I went to Lutheran Bible Institute, I enjoyed studying. My classes were actual studies of the Bible books, parish education classes and missionary studies. I wanted to learn. With this desire, I focused on studying. It was at Bible school that I learned how to study. One of my classes was titled, "How to Study."

I did well at LBI, which enabled me to go to college. I applied at Cascade College in Portland, Oregon. They not only looked at my high school grades, they also considered how I did at Bible school. They accepted my credits. I was able to enroll as a sophomore in college, but it was in name only, because I decided to major in elementary education and I needed a four-year program to graduate with a Bachelor of Science degree.

While I was at Cascade College, Patsy was attending Willamette University in Salem, Oregon. We communicated via letters:

October 2, 1965

Dear Patsy,

I'm in the school library, as usual at this time of day. I have an English Lit class in thirty-five minutes. I just returned from lunch. Before lunch, I read the "Nun's Priest's Tale" by Chaucer. It was very interesting. I read it in a modern translation from a library book. Now I have to read it from my text book. I find it quite impossible because it's written in Middle English. "A povre widwe, somdel stape in age," which means, "A poor widow, somewhat advanced in age,"

I got your last letter. I was sure glad to hear that you once again gained your study mood. How is it now? Mine's kind of at an in between stage - up high one minute and down the next. I plan to take drastic action though.

Prayer from Psalm 90: "So teach us to number our days that we may gain a heart of wisdom."

Dear Patsy,

I'm in the library right now. I should be studying, but I started to get a little sleepy. I don't dare close my eyes. I didn't go to bed at all last night. I wrote and typed a twelve page term paper. I finished it. I wish you were here to correct all the grammar errors for me. I guess I don't wish that because if you did I would probably have to re-type the whole thing.

I've had my contacts in for thirty hours, without taking them out of my eyes. I can see fine. Pretty good, eh?

Dear Linda,

I have to give an hour report in my German class Wednesday night, which I haven't started yet, let alone doing my research and I'm absolutely petrified. Then next Wednesday, I have a two hour report in Psychology of Religion. Alas! So I will get back to work. God be with you.

Love, Patsy

Often, Patsy and I wrote about our thoughts and ideas and we shared books that were meaningful.

Dear Patsy,

The sun is shining and the birds are chirping. I feel good. Isn't it good to feel good? I wish I felt this great all the time. Of course, if one felt good all the time there would be no contrast between feeling good and not feeling good so one would never know when he or she was feeling good. A person would probably only know if they felt more good than they felt before.

One of the books Patsy shared with me was "The Prophet" by Kahlil Gibran. Gibran lived before our time, 1883 - 1931; however, his message was popular during our late teen years. Patsy refers to him in one of our philosophical discussion letters.

Dear Linda,

That's interesting, what you said about if you felt good all the time there would be no contrast between good and bad and you wouldn't know if you were feeling good. I think, there's a passage in The Prophet, on joy and sorrow. It says, the height of your joy will only be as high as the depth of your sorrow or something like that.

Gibran's exact words: "...the selfsame well from which your laughter rises was oftentimes filled with your tears. And how else can it be? The deeper that sorrow carves into your being, the more joy you can contain."

Dear Patsy,

I just finished my last final - what a wonderful feeling of freedom! I had only one test today. Besides, being a nervous wreck all week, I lived through it. When I think of three more years of this... well, it's just one of those thoughts I can't dwell on too long.

You asked me, in one of your previous letters, what I thought about thinking in words. Well, up to this time, I haven't had the chance to think about thinking in words, but I will try to now even though my brain is currently at its weakest point. From awareness of my thoughts, I've reached the conclusion that I do think in words. The questions concerning this issue are: do babies think in words, if one had no language would one still be able to think? I think, that every human thinks whether he has a language, as we know of a language, or if he thinks in another form, not a word language, but a language expressed by feelings, instinct, etc... instead of words. Do animals think? How do they think? Does a dog think, "Bow, Wow" which translated means? What does quack, quack mean? Well, I suppose I'm way off the subject now. I've learned from experience of writing essays I'm really good at writing off the subject.

Now that I've expressed my opinion on nothing, but a big question, may I be so honored by knowing your opinion? If you are too busy to write it, you can explain it during Christmas vacation. Maybe, we'll solve the issue by New Year's.

Love, Linda

Patsy and I often tried to send mental messages. If I had not communicated with her for a period of about two weeks, I would dream about her.

Dear Patsy,

The other night I dreamt about you. I dreamed that you were walking down the street and I was so surprised to see you. I said, "Pat! Hi!" Then you laughed, your usual casual laugh, and you looked at me and said, "I'm not Pat."

Then I said, "Yes, you are, you're Pat!" Then you said, "You are mistaken!" That was the end of that dream.

Then I dreamed that I was going to visit you and you were living in a huge old apartment with apartment number 58. So I went to the apartment building and looked at all of the room numbers. There was 56, 57, and 59, but no room 58. So I thought I was mistaken. I decided your room must be number 54, but alas about the time I arrived at room 54, I woke up!

Dear Patsy,

I sent you some mental messages this last week. Did you get any of them? They were mostly messages concerning finals. I felt so sorry for myself that I felt equally sorry for anyone in the same predicament as I was experiencing.

Patsy was three years closer to college graduation than I was. She was one year older than I and she started college right after high school while I spent two years at Bible school.

Our letters encouraged us to keep studying and continue to keep plugging along.

******

Sometimes partial knowledge can be dangerous. Waiting for a disaster and being in a possible destructive path is never a good idea.

A Bad Idea

"Linda, Linda, where are you?" My mother frantically yelled my name. At the time I was three and a half years old. I had not wandered off; I was right where my mother expected me to be, playing in the front yard. She held my baby brother and ran toward me in a state of panic. She grabbed my arm with her free hand and held me close to her. I don't think I was scared; yet I knew my mom was scared.

The ground shook and there was a loud roaring noise. It sounded like the vibration of a huge truck coming down the hill. There was no truck. The noise came from beneath the earth.

We were in Portland, Oregon on April 13, 1949. We experienced a 7.1 earthquake. The haunting memory of my mother's panic reaction has stayed with me all of these years. I can still sense the tension of her holding me tight, as if I had just missed being harmed. This wasn't my only earthquake experience, but it was my first.

On another April day, sixteen years later, when I was nineteen years old, I had a similar fearful experience. It was near spring break at Lutheran Bible Institute, in Seattle, Washington during the year 1965. I was a student there enjoying all of my classes. The class I liked best was the Bible book study of James, taught by Pastor Stime. He had a way of making every lesson exciting. His teaching style was to literally run from one side of the blackboard to the other side as he made an outline emphasizing the points that he thought should be underlined. "What is your life? For you are a mist that appears for a little time and then vanishes." He continued his quote, "Instead, you ought to say, "If the Lord wills, we shall live and we shall do this or that." James 4:14-15

My graduation date was near. My only concern about life was college plans for next fall. I was so comfortable at LBI that I didn't want to even think about graduation. Every minute of my time at Bible school was precious. I just wanted it to continue forever.

111

Spring break was only a week away. I knew I had several assignments to complete, but I wasn't worried. I planned to finish my lessons during the week just in time to be able to take the train home to Portland. I looked forward to seeing Patsy. She was coming home from Salem, Oregon, taking her spring break from Willamette University.

Patsy and I did not have definite plans. Often we agreed on spontaneous decisions that would lead to what we would refer to as "adventures." I didn't realize it then, but one of our adventures I would look back on with concern. It would be years later that I realized that during one of our spring breaks we had put ourselves in a very dangerous position.

Now at LBI, I was comfortably seated in the individual arm desk chair in the classroom. Pastor Stime looked directly at us and we listened. "Look at verse two of chapter one" he started to explain. "James is talking about various trials. Think about troubles we face in life. How frustrating are life's hardships? Going through difficult times can cause anxiety, depression, and fearfulness to the point that we can question our faith. James says, 'Count it all joy - JOY' he says!" Pastor Stime continued to emphasize his point. "Count it all joy when you meet trials? Why would James say that going through trials should be a time of joy? How can we gain joy during a time of misery?"

I had my notebook open and a pencil in my right hand. I knew Pastor Stime wasn't going to wait for an answer. He continued on with his outline and any minute he would write on the blackboard a main point that would give the answer. Usually his tests consisted of filling in the blanks that he had illustrated on the board; only at test time the board would be erased, so I was paying close attention.

All of a sudden, we heard this loud roaring noise. It sounded like a jet plane booming overhead. Pastor Stime stopped talking. He stood staring at his attentive students. Then everything started to shake. The desks were moving, and the long florescent ceiling lights were sway-ing. I think we all recognized that this was an earthquake; however, we did not put into action any of the procedures from former earth-quake practice drills, like hiding under desks or tables or covering our heads. Instead, it was a stark moment of panic. The panic set our bod-ies in motion. With the exception of one student, all of us, including our teacher, dashed out the door to the outside yard. One male student stood under the archway of the main door, the place he thought would be the safest, most secure part of the structure. The rest of us feared the collapse of the building and dashed outside.

We felt no safer being outdoors. The swaying sensation continued. I had experienced other slight quakes since my first 1949 episode, and usually the shaking would only last a second or two. This time the movement continued longer. I stood on the lawn watching the ground sway beneath me. The fence alongside the adjacent field rocked and moved back and forth like a toy rocking horse.

The whole time I had been at LBI I felt secure and safe, even dur-ing the first year when there was the national tragedy of John F. Ken-nedy's death; however, when the earthquake struck, panic and fear took over. We were all helpless. The earth was weakening. The very ground supporting buildings, fences, roads and our feet was no longer reliable.

Finally, the shaking stopped. We did not return to the classroom. We all met in the administration building where the radio was tuned to the Seattle news station. "We interrupt our programming to announce that an earthquake has been felt throughout all of Western Washington including reports of tremors felt as far as British Columbia and parts of Idaho and Montana. This earthquake has a magnitude of 6.5. It began with 'loud earth noises' and then shaking that lasted over forty-five seconds. We will continue giving updates as reports come in."

We were advised to partner up with another student for the rest of the day in case there was after shock activity. It was a scary feeling. I remember being continually nervous.

Afterward, we noticed damage. There was a house where I and another girl student were doing housekeeping work. When we went to our part-time job this house, adjacent to a grass hillside, was much closer to the hillside. The grass knoll had lost part of the land area in a downward slide which set the house closer to the edge. There were some noticeable cracks in the cement area of our school and some damage done to the walls; however, most of the damage around us was minor.

When the week was over, I did go home for spring break. Patsy had a list of ideas of what we should do during our free time. "We could get our accordions and practice some songs, we could go hiking out by Multnomah Falls, or ride our bikes out to the airport or..." her voice raised in excitement, "or go to a Beatnik Coffee House and learn about Beatniks, and I just happen to know of one."

I already guessed the answer, but I asked the question anyway, "One certain beatnik or one coffee house?" I figured she wanted to see her friend Dave.

I didn't wait for her answer I just asked the next question, "Are you talking about a particular Beatnik House?"

"Well," Patsy admitted, "We could do some things this afternoon and then this evening go and hear him play. It might be interesting."

I didn't know much about Beatnik coffee houses, nor did I drink any coffee, even any different types of coffee; yet I thought this would be an interesting experience.

We arrived at the coffee house about 9:30 p.m. This was not a house, but rather a large cement building in Portland and we were on the lower floor. There were round tables with chairs and young people surrounding the floor space. A bar with espresso coffee machines was against the back wall with waiters in jeans standing around. The room was dimly lit and fogged with smoke. It took several minutes for Dave and Patsy to make eye contact.

Dave was on the stage strumming his guitar and reciting poetry. He had long, auburn hair and wore tight jeans and a white shirt with gold threads entwined on the collar and on the long sleeves. Patsy and I were wore cutoff jeans and shirts that were hanging out over our waist, trying to look as casual as we could for this outing.

When he did notice us, he yelled to the chatting audience, with his lips close to the microphone, "Hey, loosen up everybody. I got some visiting friends. I'm going to dedicate this next song to Patsy and Linda." I was surprised that he included my name because he really was Patsy's friend. The crowd quieted down.

Then to the background beat of a bongo drum played by his band partner, and the chords of his guitar, he slowly drawled out a poem about sunflowers, shade, whisky and parades. It had a neat rhyme, but I really didn't understand the whole message.

I ordered hot buttered rum coffee, that I slowly sipped, but I really didn't like the flavor.

This was my first taste of the Beatnik era. Patsy seemed to enjoy this experience with more enthusiasm than I was feeling. The echoing poetry seemed to send a repeated message:

Woe's Me

The drumbeat is the key
Protesting on the land
Viet Nam, the Klu Klux Klan
Flowers pressed in your hair
The rhythm in the air

LSD, grassy weeds
Tattoos, long chains of beads
Late hours, night time bands
Freedom is what we seek
Do you hear the heart beat?

Even though Dave was into the Beatnik scene as far as his music and chanting poetry went, I didn't think he was into drugs, drinking or even smoking. He always preached the clean earthy style way of living. He treated Patsy and me with flattery and respect. He came to our table and hugged and greeted us like long lost friends. "It is so cool that you gals came. Do you like the drinks and rhymes?"

Patsy enthusiastically praised the coffee. "I love the flavor of this; it tastes like fresh caramel with a hint of vanilla coffee bean. I also love listening to you play the guitar and how you almost sing your poetry. It's nice to see you Dave. What's been happening?"

"Well, I'm taking classes at Portland State and I've got several gigs lined up. What about you two?"
Pasty responded first, "I'm still at Willamette, majoring in Psychology and minoring in German and wondering what I'll do after college."

Then Dave turned toward me. I decided not to go into detail about attending Bible School; it just didn't seem like the time to discuss religion, God or the Bible, or to give my opinion about the coffee, which I thought, tasted like mud. So I changed the subject, "I just experienced the earthquake in Seattle, last week."

"Wow, cool!" Then Dave reflected on memories of our last time together. "Do you gals remember the last time we saw each other? We spent the afternoon at Seaside Beach."

I had not thought about it, but I did remember the last time we were together. It was in March 1964 right after the Alaskan Quake. Patsy had called me and told me they were headed for the beach and asked if I would like to tag along. I was always ready to go to the beach so I quickly agreed. I didn't realize then what their purpose was.

The news at the time was that a tsunami might hit the Pacific coastline right after the Alaskan Quake. We were on spring break then too. Dave and Patsy were going to the beach to see the high expected waves.

I knew little about tsunamis, only enough information to clarify the fact that it would be dangerous to stick our toes in the ocean when a tsunami was predicated. So on the north side of Seaside, where there were few people and a long area of sand, we sat on the last edge of the sand, near the paved road. From a distance we watched the waves rolling into shore and sliding back out to sea.

Dave had his guitar. We sat on the beach for hours with the smell of the fresh salty air and the feel of the cool shore breeze blowing through our hair.

We talked and listened while Dave strummed his guitar chords. We harmonized and sang tunes from "Kum Ba Yah Lord" to "We'll Sing in the Sunshine."

"You know," I said to Patsy and Dave, "we are lucky to be alive." If a tidal wave or tsunami really would have hit Seaside on that particular day we could have possibly died. That was rather stupid on our part thinking we could outrun a wave. I've heard they can come miles inland."

"Well," Patsy sighed, "our disappointment of not seeing high waves was really our blessing."

Dave took Patsy's left hand and then he held my right hand. "It would have been a lovely way to die though, my guitar, two beauti- ful gals and the ocean waves." We smiled and agreed, although I was thinking life was more for me than the freedom of the sea or the beat sound of the dark coffee houses. Secretly I was thanking the Lord that I lived safely through several earthquakes, and on that day, at the beach, it was a time of peaceful waves.

That night I read in the book of James the last part of Pastor Stime's lecture: "Count it all joy, my breathen, when you meet various trials, for you know that the testing of your faith produces steadfastness. And let steadfastness have its full effects, that you may (mature) be perfect and complete, lacking in nothing." James 1:2-4

******

Life has a way of taking our goals and fulfilling them or changing our goals. Sometimes it all depends on what we decide or how fate determines our path.

Indecision

At an early age my future plans and goals were clear. Patsy's future plans and goals were not. In high school she learned about a man named Albert Schweitzer. His life consisted of ideals that she too wanted to achieve.

Albert Schweitzer was a German humanitarian and a man of many talents. His gifts varied from being a philosopher, pastor, musician (organist) and physician. His purpose in life was to serve his fellow man. He studied medicine and then practiced in Africa. It was there that he used the natives to help him build a hospital in a remote area that previously did not have medical services. At the hospital he worked during the day and at night he wrote books. These books were the financial support for the hospital program. In 1952 he won the Nobel Peace Prize. Patsy had hopes of some day meeting this hero.

It was during her last year of college when that hope became a possible reality. She decided to apply for the Peace Corps and to work in Africa. Unfortunately, Albert Schweitzer died in the year 1965. Patsy received her acceptance notice to the Peace Corps on May 12, 1966.

Dear Linda,

This Peace Corps thing has really got me walking around in the clouds. I got a telegram Saturday morning. I read it and just stood around looking at it for the longest time. I'm supposed to start training June 20 at the University of North Carolina for a project in Malawi. Malawi is in SE Africa. It was called Nyasaland until just two years ago when it gained its independence from England.

I feel like a chicken just about ready to hatch out of its egg and start living. It will be hard to leave the warm security of school, but it will be exciting to see what life has to offer. God bless you.

Love, Patsy

Patsy went to North Carolina and she lived in the dorm at the University of North Carolina. There were about fifty Peace Corps students learning Nyanga, the language of Malawi, and studying the country's history, culture and even the music of the people. For years afterwards Patsy would remember one song called, "Kwatcha Malawi" that translates to "Wake up, Malawi" a new day is here, meaning "hurry we have our independence now."

During her training there were natives from the country who were their teachers. One of their future assignments involved taking a census in many of the African villages and doing public health work, which included giving Tb skin tests.

Their practical training was to go out in the country area of North Carolina. They were dropped in groups of pairs. On bicycles they went to the farms amongst the poor black people. They charted the number of people and recorded how they were related to others in the community. Patsy loved this experience. She commented about how friendly the people were and how they invited them into their homes and shared with them of what they had. She told about one incident when she was sitting in one of the homes with a family and they gave her and her fellow workers water to drink. They only had one Mason jar that they passed around and all took a drink. And she attended a church where she was the only white person there. She said, "Everyone treated me nice."

At the end of the training they were sent back home and had ten days to pack and to leave for Malawi.

When the day came to catch her flight to Africa, Patsy was undecided about going or staying. Her luggage was packed, she had her shots, and her passport was complete. She sat in her parents' kitchen weighing the pros and cons. No one else could decide her future for her. It had to be her decision and yet, she was influenced by others.

Her parents often encouraged her to seek her own avenues of interest, except they were not happy about the idea of her living in the faraway country of Africa, and working for the Peace Corps.

Her steady boyfriend, Marty, did not want her to go. He wanted to marry her and encouraged her to "settle down" and raise a family. The team she had worked with in North Carolina had some frictions too. A few people that she met in North Carolina did not stay with the Peace Corps. One of the teachers from Africa, whom she had grown fond of, went back before the training period had ended, so there were conflicts that tore apart the cohesion of the group. The enthusiasm and energy that was first initiated had waned. There might have been the fear, too, that if she really went to Africa it would change her life completely. Maybe in her heart she knew if she went to Africa she wouldn't return home to her comfortable lifestyle. Africa and its needs, its cry for help, its culture and lifestyle changes might hold her there. Maybe that threat was lingering in the back of her mind because she had a love for the land and its people before she was even there. Patsy had a huge, burdensome decision to make. Should she head to the airport, as planned, or stay within the walls of her home, the safety. and stability of what she knew best?

We sat in the kitchen and discussed the issues. "I could get on this plane and go to Africa. I think I want to go to Africa. Marty is saying he won't wait for me to return. He doesn't even care if I only stay one year or if I do the two year term. He said, 'We're finished if you go to Africa.' So Linda, what do I do with that?"

I thought about Patsy and Marty. I liked them both. They seemed so perfect for each other. They were creative, fun people with a natural love for life, animals, and an easy lifestyle. Marty was a good, honest, hard-working man. Most importantly, he deeply loved Patsy.

I sighed, "I don't know. Are you interested in Marty being your future husband or are you just satisfied with him being your steady boyfriend?"

Patsy realized she needed to answer this question, not for me, but for herself so she attacked the puzzlement of her own thoughts. "That's a good question and I don't know the answer. I just can't imagine myself settling down with one person and staying home and raising children. I'm not ready for that. I want to do more. What the more is I don't know."

"Well, even husbands and wives sometimes do more. You would just have a partner, and as a team you'd have goals."

Patsy raised her voice in frustration, "That too, is part of my problem. Marty doesn't want to do the more that I want to do. He's happy with his new piece of property and his goal of having his own print shop. He doesn't want to go anywhere. He just wants to settle down."

"Okay," I suggested, "Let's leave Marty out of the picture, if he wasn't even involved in this decision would you go to Africa?"

Patsy hesitated, "That's my dilemma; I just don't know. I was ready to go when I finished the course in North Carolina, but then I came home. Mom and Dad are not excited about me going. They are worried and just aren't happy that I plan to do this. It is like they think I should be doing something here not in Africa. Also, I wonder if this is the right decision. This is a major life change and I just don't know if this is right for me."

I was always one to solve problems and to arrive at some solution or conclusion, so I continued.

"All right, let's take out your parents' hesitation. Now we only have you and you alone. Forget me too, because I really want you to stay around. If Patsy was in this world all alone with no one else's opinion but her own, what would she do?"

Patsy was near tears. "Here is my frustration. I feel something. It's as if someone is calling me to do something important with my life, to go somewhere, to have a definite purpose and to help others in some way; however, I don't feel I'm ready to go to Africa. I feel it is a major change and I'm just not ready for that commitment. I don't think I can go to Africa right now."

So we sat there for another hour, until it was too late to go to the airport. Patsy heard a plane fly over the house; she lived within a few miles from the Portland airport, and when she heard the roar of the engine she shared with me her thought. "You know, Linda, that plane could be the very plane that I was supposed to be on."

I sensed her sadness and realized that her life goal of going to Africa, her desire of helping those in need among the African people, was not going to happen. This was a missed opportunity, so I promised her the only compromise I could think of at the time.

"Don't unpack your bags Patsy. We will go somewhere. This week we will take a trip. So don't unpack."

Then I went home and asked my dad for the use of his car, a '51 Mercury, for one week. I was planning a week of vacation and travel time with Patsy. My dad agreed, especially after I gave him elaborate details about how upset Patsy was from missing her flight and maybe her chance of a life time. He agreed with one stipulation. We could use the car and go for a trip, but we were not to leave the state of Oregon. I was thinking more like heading to California. I called Patsy and told her that on Saturday we would leave, not to another country, but for an escape from disappointing indecision and for a tour of our state of Oregon.

******

"Westward ho," except we didn't go west we headed east.

Central Oregon

"For this trip we will need an electric frying pan. With a frying pan we can save money and eat our meals in the motel room."

Patsy agreed. I already had an electric frying pan, so it was no problem. I plopped it in the bottom of the suitcase. I reasoned if I carried the suitcase I could bring it into the motel room without the manager even noticing. I wasn't too sure how he (or she) would appreciate the idea of our cooking meals in a room that would probably be minus a kitchen.

We decided that any canned foods would work with the electric pan to heat our dinner. So we gathered what can goods we could find in Patsy family's kitchen and in my parents' pantry, like spaghetti, chili, and pork and beans.

I was excited that we were going on a trip. Patsy might have lacked some of the same enthusiasm I felt; after all, she had just turned down an airplane ride to Africa and a career in a foreign country. I didn't have any such plans so driving a hundred or so miles down the road sounded inviting.

We packed the car and stuffed an unfolded (it was too difficult to fold correctly) Oregon map in the glove box. Near ten a.m. (no point rushing early since we didn't really have a plan or destination) we left home. As soon as we settled in the front seat of my dad's 51 Mercury, Patsy started singing one of our favorite traveling songs: "I love to go a-wandering along the mountain track, And as I go I love to sing, My knap sack on my back." We sang all four verses on our way to our first stop - the familiar Multnomah Falls.

Often my friends and I drove to the falls. We'd hike to the top, beyond the Benson Foot Bridge, to the highest point. One time, with a church group, I hiked further because we didn't start at the falls, but instead we were about three or four miles from the falls and then hiked over rough terrain just to get to the falls. It was a beautiful area.

Being there gave me a sense of nature's control over the universe. If the 611' falls were consistently flowing over the banks, it was proof that the world was on its normal, steady course, and life was good.

Patsy and I could not resist the urge so we stopped and took time to hike up to the Benson Bridge. We lingered on the bridge watching the water spray over the rocks. Then we hiked back down to the lodge and relaxed with ice cream cones and ice water drinks.

Then I drove up the twisting road to Crown Point to see the Vista House. As soon as we got out of the car we felt the brisk wind blowing our hair and pushing against our bodies. The day was warm so the breeze felt pleasant. Then we climbed up the stairs, in the Vista House, to see the surrounding view. The Vista House was a huge empty stone building with only a restroom inside. Some called it an expensive outhouse. The view was a thirty-five-mile stretch of the Columbia River on the Oregon side and views of the Washington side. It was a landmark built for the pioneers. We felt somewhat like pioneers venturing through Oregon territory.

As we left Crown Point, I asked Patsy, "Have you ever been to Kah Nee Ta Indian Reservation?"

As if going to Africa, Kah Nee Ta was advertised as going to another nation. The resort opened in 1964, complete with overnight camping facilities in teepees or cabins. There were Warm Spring swimming pools and also horses to ride. The warm water swimming pools sounded especially inviting.

Patsy was familiar with Kah Nee Ta; her family had been there before. My family had gone by it before so I was thrilled to go and experience a night on an Indian Reservation.

We didn't have any prearranged reservations for our plans. When we arrived they told us the teepees were filled for the night, but there was a cabin available. The cabins were in a long row, each cabin sharing a wall with the next cabin.

Once we were settled in the cabin, we went swimming and then hiked around the desert of dry sage bush.

There was a sense of peacefulness at this reservation. It was miles off the main highway and we felt far away from the civilized busy city life. The night was extremely quiet and dark with only beauty brightness from the stars and the sound of distant coyotes.

We were lying in the twin size bunk beds, in the cabin getting ready to fall asleep; but we weren't settling down. Instead, we continued to talk and laugh uncontrollably. Patsy and I always found subjects to discuss, from deep issues like God, creation, future plans, afterlife, school subjects, daily observations, to the history and unfairness of the Indians. We wondered out loud how mineral water in a pool could be so warm, where our next road stop would be. Then we talked about the mundane issues: these beds are too hard, there could be a rattle snake in this cabin, and we listed possibilities of who might be in the next cabin. Well, we got our answer. All of a sudden we heard this rough sounding male voice shouting, "Shut up in there!"

Patsy came from a quiet, conservative, mild-mannered family and she was shocked. Shocked that anyone would yell such a command in the middle of the night, but also she was totally disbelieving that the order was addressed to us.

"You don't think he is yelling at us do you?" She innocently asked.

I said, "Yes, that is exactly what I think."

We both agreed to quiet down. We were away from home, away from our parents, and making our own decisions, but obviously there were still restrictions even on our get-away and escape vacation.

The next day we left Warm Springs. I suggested we go into Redmond, Oregon and visit a site that I remembered as a child. I had fond memories of castles, statues and fancy rock displays at Petersen's Rock Garden. This garden was designed by one man named, Rasmus Petersen. He was from Denmark and he wanted to give a gift to his new country America. He used the rocks of the surrounding Central Oregon land and built a miniature village consisting of small castles, water falls, a swan lake and ornamental rock agate bridges and a small scale Statue of Liberty with the plaque saying, "Enjoy yourself, it is later than you think."

When we arrived, it was still attractive, but rather odd to realize that the rock structures seemed smaller than my childhood image.

I suggested the next stop be at my Aunt and Uncle's home in Bend where I figured we could get a free night's lodging. My Uncle Leonard and my Aunt Lillian had five kids: Donald, Randy, Mike, Dennis and one girl named Judy. I especially admired Judy. She was older than I and very pretty with blond curly hair. She was very kind. Judy spoke in a soft voice and I wanted to be more like her.

My sister, Susan, had given me directions to my Uncle and Aunt's farm house. So I just followed her written map. We went off the main highway down this gravel country path, Alfalfa Market Road. The cows and horses were off in the fields and we parked in front of the barn. The house was off to the right. Before I went to the door, I decided to give Patsy a warning.

I recalled, from my early childhood visits, my Uncle and Aunt being very gracious hosts – welcoming my family with happy greetings, dinner and overnight hospitality. My sister did remind me though that Uncle Leonard liked to yell a lot and we shouldn't be surprised about how he might greet me.

I was never aware of his yelling, but also I never went to his house uninvited before and without my parents along, so I wasn't sure what to expect.

I decided I better warn Patsy, "I don't know what kind of greeting we might get here. So don't be surprised if my Uncle says something rather harsh – really my Aunt and Uncle are wonderful people."

Pasty wondered out loud, "You mean like the late night command we got last night at the cabin?"

"Yeah, maybe just like that."

I opened the screen door and knocked on the front door. Uncle Leonard opened the door. There was silence for a moment like he was trying to figure out who we were and where we were from. Then he yelled, "What the hell are you doing here?"

I was very thankful I had warned Patsy.

Uncle Leonard opened the door wider. "Well, don't just stand there, come on in." Then he turned to Aunt Lillian. "Lillian, add two table settings. We've got company for dinner."

Leonard and Lillian lived in a country farm house. They used a pump to pump water into their kitchen sink. Their bathroom was an outhouse. Their milk was from a cow in the barn, the eggs came from the nearby chicken coop, and their vegetables from their garden. It was much different from the city life that I knew.

Their kids were always busy working. The only time the family sat together was at meals or in the evenings when they gathered by the wood stove and told stories. This was my favorite part about visiting them.

That night Patsy and I slept in a big poster double bed. We did not talk late into the night. This family would be up at the sound of the morning rooster.

The next day my cousin, Don, saddled up two horses, Old Blue and Silver. He told us we could ride them around the fenced field.

Riding horses was a special treat because the only time I went riding was in Bend or the few times I rode a rented horse on one hour guided trips at the beach.

Don gave us a few quick instructions then slapped the horse's behind and let us enjoy the ride. Amazingly, my horse actually moved as I directed the reins to left or right. I practiced standing in the stirrups as Old Blue galloped across the field.

I figured he knew best when to stop and when to slow down. I discovered I didn't bounce nearly as much when I stood in the stirrups and I could save myself a side ache. Patsy was more used to riding, than I was, she had taken horse-back riding lessons, so she was doing fine, completely relaxed on her horse.

Late that afternoon we said our goodbyes. Aunt Lillian filled up a bag of baked cookies and muffins for us to take along.

Uncle Leonard directed me to take a short cut home, up around Sisters, staying off the main highway. He said, "Take this more scenic trip."

We followed his directions, but later, when I told my sister about the experience and she mentioned it to Uncle Leonard he denied ever telling us about that mountainous road. The road was narrow, and the signs kept indicting sharp curves and limited speeds from fifteen miles per hour to five miles per hour with signs saying, "Slow, Caution."

I was busy watching the narrow road and anticipating the next hazardous curve – so busy that I missed most of the forest and mountain views. For me it was the most harrowing, longest short cut I had ever driven. Why, my uncle denied telling me about it I still don't know. I certainly did not find it on my own.

We went through Sweet Home just because we liked the inviting name of the town and we enjoyed seeing the quaint-covered bridges.

We kept driving and made it into Albany. We spent the night in Albany. It was there we used our frying pan and had a late dinner of pork and beans.

Our days and money were running out. We headed back to Portland, stopping at Multnomah Falls once again to renew our energy.

This wasn't a major trip, and it wasn't a complete cure for indecision or disappointment, but it definitely was a diversion. For Patsy, it was a stepping stone to another adventure for her life. She changed her course not immediately, but after several months of taking classes to become a medical technologist, she bought a car and did what she wanted to do most, travel. She got in her vehicle and drove beyond Oregon searching for whatever experiences might come her way.

******

There was one college experience where Nancy helped me with her secretarial skills.

School Struggles

After high school Nancy went on short mission trips. She also
got a job as a secretary working for the Youth for Christ organiza-
tion. While she worked there I attended Cascade College. There was
one evening when Nancy helped me with my college essay. I had
a female English teacher that I wasn't too fond of. Just like in high
school, I still had a stubborn attitude. This teacher was insistent that
we memorize a particular Bible verse, II Timothy 2:15 "Do your best
to present yourself to God as one approved, a workman who has no
need to be ashamed, rightly handling the word of truth." I already
had it memorized in the Revised Standard Version. I saw no reason
to change the words I already had clear in my mind. She insisted we
memorize the same verse in the King James Version: "Study to shew
thyself approved unto God, a workman that needth not to be ashamed,
rightly dividing the word of truth." I knew from the first day in class
that we were at odds.

She assigned us to write an essay. She wanted us to do a rough
draft and turn it in for correction and then do a rewrite. I never turned
in rough drafts; I only turned in what I thought was my final copy. So
I decided to do my very best on my "rough draft." I wrote my paper.
I corrected my paper. I looked up as many words as I questioned for
correct spelling (there was no spell check in those days) and then I
reread my paper, and reread it, and thought it was ok. Then I took it
to my friend Nancy. After hours, when her work day was over, Nancy
and I went to the Youth for Christ Office. Then on Nancy's fancy,
much more sophisticated typewriter than what I had, Nancy typed my
paper with perfect margins, commas in the correct places and sentences with strict grammar rules applied.

The next day I turned in my "rough draft." I knew it was a good,
impressive essay. Well, this English teacher looked at my paper and
read it carefully and then she took her red marker and drew a line
at the bottom of each page and told me it was a rough draft. Then
she said I needed to retype it, and turn it in again. I couldn't believe

it. She didn't find one error on that essay, yet she drew a line on my paper so I would have to retype it.

Of course I didn't own that fancy typewriter at the Youth for Christ office and I wasn't about to ask Nancy to spend another late evening with me to retype that error- free essay. I was devastated. I just turned the paper back in - red lines on the bottom and accepted a lower grade than the A that I deserved. I didn't rememorize the Bible verse either. I knew I was right and she was wrong.

******

Even though Nancy acted so hesitant about rough conditions at Camp Colton, years before, she ventured beyond her comfort zone years later while on mission trips.

A Desperate Call in the Amazon

Written by Nancy G. Spencer

It was mid-morning as our two vehicles stopped at our remote destination. There wasn't even a hint of civilization for hundreds of miles except for a dilapidated old road. The scenery was incredibly lush green on all sides with the rise of hills before us.

I thought to myself, "How did this all happen?" Here I am in my 20's, deep in the Amazon Jungle, over four thousand miles from my home in Portland, Oregon! I volunteered as an administrative support worker for a commitment of six months at the Summer Institute of Linguistics in Yarinachocha, Peru.

The institute was comprised of other volunteer workers, like myself, to help support talented linguists from around the world. These linguists were completely dedicated to the cause of helping the Amazonian Indians become literate and to translate the Bible into over forty-five different tribal dialects in Peru. I had been in Peru for only a few months, but already the experiences I gained were beyond my wildest thoughts. I was a different person in many ways.

This weekend six other people had joined me for a long-awaited break for a few hours away from the daily commitments we each had back at the institute. The difference of the climate was already noticeable as were in the jungle foothills. The cooling refreshment from the usual intense heat and humidity was most welcomed.

We quickly set up our tents to camp out for the weekend. We camped near a narrow river that was bubbling along with the background sounds of the loud, melodic jungle. The beauty of the jungle surrounding us was breathtaking including the massive waterfall only a short distance away.

133

Soon we would all take a small trek around this thundering wall of water, as the splendor of the environment was irresistible. We anticipated a fun adventure.

After lunch we started hiking along the steep slopes high above the torrential waterfall. The deafening sound of the falls blocked out any other sounds. Conversation with each other was impossible.

We were each deep into our own thoughts trying to find adequate footing along the rocky path. Sometimes the rocks were a bit slippery because of the moist air from the falls. We were spaced several yards from each other and moving along in single file. I was the last person in the row of hikers.

Then it happened! Suddenly, without any warning, I lost my footing completely. I started slipping on some unnoticed mossy coating on the sheet of rock beneath my feet.

I began to slide down the hillside directly toward the waterfall. There was nothing to grab onto. My feet were fumbling for footing.

My thoughts were this can't be happening and me with no swimming ability. I probably won't be able to survive the deep plunge into the pounding waterfall anyway. I cried out to the Lord, "Save me."

Just as quickly as I lost my footing all of a sudden I stopped sliding downhill. How I stopped is amazing as there wasn't anything that I could see to stop the sliding motion.

A verse from Psalms flooded into my mind: "The Lord God delivers my soul from death and my feet from stumbling." Ps. 116:8

After several attempts I finally got the attention of the other hikers. Then it was decided to turn back and not go any further.

In a short time we returned back to the safety of our tents. Back at the campsite we all gathered around discussing what had happened. I was still shaking from the close call just moments earlier. Someone mentioned that over the past years eight people had drowned in that beautiful waterfall.

******

Patsy and I made some plans that never worked out.

Fate or Plans

Fate has a way of changing our plans. It was back in January, 1969 when Patsy and I were miles apart, but thinking very similar thoughts. I was in my last year of college and this is what Patsy wrote:

Dear Linda,

I have something very significant to talk about in this letter. It's an exciting subject! It's about our future! Would you like to be my roommate starting next fall or sooner if possible? I don't have any idea about what I'm doing this summer, but I'm especially concerned about next year. I know this is extremely early for you to make any decisions, but job interviews starts this month so I have to decide where I want a job.

There are a lot of possibilities so if you are interested in living in some particular area for a whole school year and if you would like to live with me just clue me in. Ok? Ok!

Mostly the interviews are in Oregon, but I could get interviews for California, Alaska, Montana, Washington, New Mexico, Hawaii and I could write to other places too.

During this same month Patsy, who already graduated from college, was living in Richmond, Virginia. She was working as a lab technician for a chemical company, but the company closed down. It was late one night when she got the idea of becoming a teacher and possibly being my roommate.

She also offered me this exciting summer plan:

About this summer, I think I will be back at Sea Island. So if you would like to spend your summer at a beautiful resort hotel on the lovely southern Georgia Coast amidst the lush palm trees, bathing in the warm surf, basking in the radiant sun, there's a place waiting for you in the employment of the Cloister Hotel.

The money is good. You could fly down and ride back with me around August. Living facilities are no problem because you could live in the dorm. Transportation is no problem because you live and work in the same building and the beach is only two blocks away. If you ever want to go anyplace, I have a car.

Dear Patsy,

Your idea of me coming to Georgia made me want to cry. You don't know how badly I want to come. Your offer for me to come was more than generous; however, my dear Patsy, I'm afraid that it is impossible for me to come this summer. If it was just impractical I would still strongly consider it.

At first I was going to summer school for the fun of it, but due to conflicts in my schedule it has become a necessity. I have one term of Biology left and it is only offered in the mornings and next year I have to take the "Junior Block Program" (teaching methods class) that is only offered in the mornings.

Don't think I didn't consider your offer. All this last week I've been trying to figure out ways to avoid reality and to just take off and join you. I've failed in figuring out a way.

These were missed opportunities and plans that never came to fruition.

I once asked myself what would happen if I asked God: "What if..."

What if I would have interviewed in one of those far away states, what if I would have gone to Georgia and spent my summer, what if

Patsy would have moved to Monmouth and taken a teaching position? How different our lives might have been.

The revelation I received in my mind - the answer God might have given was: "There are no what ifs... What was to be - was."

What is amazing is the friendship that Patsy and I experienced over the years when we were apart, when we made plans or when we spent time together without definite plans.

******

After college I started a teaching career in Longview, Washington. Then my plans changed drastically.

PART IV

OUR **ADULT** YEARS

Lies

I told three major lies in my life time. One of these lies I can still laugh about, but the other two untruths continue to haunt me. These two lies penetrated my mind so vividly that I promised myself I would never tell a major lie again.

As a young child I told my friend Patsy that I was born in Texas. It just seemed like a more exciting place to be from than my hometown Portland, Oregon.

Patsy believed me and that story never got corrected until we were adults. We were reminiscing and I confessed that I lied to her years before about my birthplace.

She asked me, in a shocked voice, "What? You weren't born in Texas?"

I replied, "No. Didn't you know that?"

Amazing how sometimes lies never get rectified. It is a joke now. Even my daughter, who travels frequently for her work, calls me often from Dallas Fort Worth International Airport in Texas just to say she's calling from my "birthplace."

I've never been to Texas, though someday I plan to see the state that supposedly I was from.

The second lie involved my girlfriend Marilyn. That lie occurred the evening of her accident, except at the time I didn't know she had an accident.

I was fifteen years old and I was babysitting for two young neighbor girls. The girls were asleep. So while waiting for their parents to come home, I called my friend Nancy. We jabbered on the phone till late in the evening.

Later when I arrived home, my parents confronted me. My mom said she tried to call me where I was working and the line was continuously busy. I did not want to admit to Mom that Nancy and I had spent over an hour on the phone, so instead I told her several calls came in from Patsy, Marilyn, and Nancy.

It was the next day when my mother was told about Marilyn's accident that she realized Marilyn had not called me on the phone. She had spent the night in the hospital. There were no phone calls from Marilyn that evening.

I was caught in a lie. So, as liars often do, I had to lie again to defend myself. I said, "No, Mom, I didn't say Marilyn, just Nancy and Patsy."

The guilt was penetrating almost as if my lie had caused Marilyn's terrible tragedy. I vowed then, "I will never tell a major lie again." I did change my ways. Even though it was easy and tempting for me to exaggerate truths, expand stories, state excuses, I really did try my best to stick to the facts.

The third deception happened during my first year of teaching. I lied, not because it was my choice, but because I was advised that it was for the best and was of necessity for me not to share the facts. So I lied. I lied to friends, family members and anyone that questioned me.

My greatest sin, in my mind, was that I lied to my dear grandmother. I know in my heart she would have accepted the truth with love and understanding, but I was told not to tell her because it might upset her too much. When she asked pertinent questions I answered with partial details and did not clarify the situation. Her look told me she didn't believe me.

My reality and my honesty were challenged during this year at the age of twenty-four. I was a third grade teacher. This career was my life's goal. I was doing exactly what I wanted to do when a man came into my life and changed my direction. This is the letter I wrote to Patsy to introduce her to him:

Dear Patsy,

I hope you are sitting down because what I have to tell you requires your undivided, relaxed attention. I don't want to shock you and have you faint on the hardwood floor.

I guess I'll start at the beginning. I think that last you knew I was dating George. As you remember, that wasn't going very well. I like him and he definitely likes me; however, he kept losing his jobs and making promises that never went anywhere. It was like I had to be a mother to him. His idea of future happiness was that I would get a great teaching job and we would be rich on my salary. I'm not too sure what his plan was for what he was going to do other than be happy watching me work.

Well, since I've been up here in Longview teaching, I've met another guy. I feel it was meant to be. As you know, Sharon and I both got teaching jobs in Kelso and an apartment in Longview. One day, as I was walking to the bus depot, to go home to Portland, this handsome, smiling, fun guy asked me if I would like a ride to the bus depot, being that he saw me walking down the road with this "heavy" suitcase. He thought it was heavy; actually it was empty, because I always went home with an empty case so I could bring more stuff back to the apartment. I was running rather late to catch the bus so I said sure, thanks! He, being the gentlemen that he is, opened the door and lifted my light-weight suitcase into the car.

I still remember the gist of our first conversation: I looked at his friendly face and decided I did need a ride and it would be okay to say yes to this offer. "I really appreciate this ride. I'm heading to Portland, where my folks live. My name is Linda."

"Hi, Linda, I'm Ron and I'm heading to the Greyhound Station."

"Oh, were you going there anyway?"

He laughed slightly and grinned, "No, but I'm going there now."

I felt like I needed to give him an explanation. "The reason I had to walk to the station was because my roommate, Sharon, has a car, but doesn't have a driver's license. I have the license, but I don't own a car."

"Well," he responded, "that's an interesting predicament."

I was anxious to tell him that I was a teacher with a third grade classroom, but I decided to give him a chance to share first. "Tell me Ron, what do you do in Longview?"

"I work at Longview Fibre – I do accounting."

I thought and said, "Very interesting,"

He was quick to change the focus back to me. "Tell me Linda, what do you do in Longview?"

"Actually, what I do I really do in Kelso; I'm a third grade teacher."

"I'm sure that is exciting."

"Yeah, every day is an adventure." Then for lack of anything else to say I repeated my information. "Yes, I live in Longview and work in Kelso."

Then Ron surprised me by saying, "I know where you live – you live in the same apartment complex that I and my roommate live in."

I was surprised. "Really?"

"Yeap, Flaskerude Apartments. Only I live in the separate unit and you live in the larger upstairs unit."

I was thinking, this guy noticed me and for some reason I didn't recognize him.

"So you've seen me before?"

"Yeah, we've noticed you gals."

"Hmmm," I mumbled. I wanted to ask more about his opinion of his observations, but decided that was enough information for now.

He stopped in front of the bus station.

I jumped out of the car and so did he. He quickly grabbed my suitcase and handed it to me. Then he said, "See you around."

I smiled and said, "Probably, beings we live next door to each other."

Then he reassured me, "I'm sure we will." Then he added for clarification, "See each other around."

And that was that.

Days later came the invitation for Sharon and me to join him and his roommate, Jim, at their apartment for a steak dinner, completely prepared by them. That was the start. From there we went to movies, more steak dinners, trips to Portland and a lot of together time.

Ron captured my heart, impressed my friends and my parents. He demonstrated love to me and affection that no other man had given to me and I returned his love.

He had some secrets from his past that would soon invade his present life. He was facing a court date and it was near. So one evening he told me a story.

"Linda, I have something I need to say to you, something that may change our relationship and might change your mind about me."

I was quick to argue, "Nothing you could say would change my mind about you and me. I love you."

"And I love you, but I need to explain to you some things about my past. First of all, I was married before."

Then he showed me a picture of a dark-haired cute boy, about the age of two.

"This is a picture of my son. My wife left me and this is how old my son was about two years ago. I haven't seen him or her these last two years because she remarried and moved to Australia. She did not want to see me again and told me I would never see my son again."

I could tell that it was very hard and emotional for Ron to even talk to me about this so I didn't question the whys or the details. I listened.

He continued, "When this all happened I went emotionally crazy. I was experiencing a nervous breakdown and I couldn't work. Instead, it was like insanity and I started doing actions that normally I would never do. This buddy and I went on a spending frenzy and we went from state to state cashing checks carelessly.

I was listening, but I couldn't see the real picture. I had known him for months and he seemed to be in control of his life. He lived in a nice apartment, worked at a steady full time job, drove a decent car, impressed my friends and relatives with proper behavior and extreme

145

politeness, and even attended church with me. This man he described didn't seem to be the same man I was in love with.

My love outweighed any precautions or warning signals for me to do anything other than to believe him and to continue loving him. My heart ached, but I just said, "I love you no matter what and I will be with you, no matter what."

That night I had no idea what that promise would cost me.

The court date arrived. I sat in a Tacoma courtroom to hear the sentence given by the judge. "Ron McCoy you have been charged with check forgery and fraudulent check transporting across the state line. You are sentenced to five years in a federal state prison." The judge slammed the gavel, indicating the sentence was final. Five years seemed like a lifetime. Ron was handcuffed and put into a cell right then and there.

After he was imprisoned, I had flu-like symptoms and I suspected that I didn't have the flu. I had morning sickness that lasted day after day continuously.

When I found out I was pregnant I hated and loved him. I hated him (wondering if he planned this to happen.) Yet, I loved him so much I longed for him to be beside me and to provide for me, and for this coming child. Instead, I was alone.

As lies often do, my lies continued like a roller coaster going up and then spiraling out of control. I wrote this letter to Patsy and it was not the total truth.

May 1970

Dear Patsy,

I have some news for you that I hope will not shock you too greatly. But before I go on if you are not sitting down please do so now. First of all, my name is no longer Linda Rose, but Linda McCoy. Ron and I are married. Now I'm wondering if I should change the subject or if you are still capable of hearing some more news!?

Ron and I have been married since December, but we didn't tell anyone because we knew my parents would not understand (since Ron and I had just met in September.) Also we didn't tell anyone because Ron had to go live in Tacoma and work and I had to stay here and teach. So we kept it a secret.

Well, this was a lie. Fortunately, unlike the lie about Texas, I did tell Patsy the whole truth shortly afterward and she was a helpful friend.

In reality, Ron and I got permission to get married. He was incarcerated at McNeil Island Prison. On April 26, 1970, he was escorted by two guards and we were married in Steilacoom, Washington in a church by a Pastor. Ron was dressed in a suit and so were the two guards. My parents attended, my friend Sharon was there, Ron's sister, brother-in-law and my brother and sister were there.

I was happy that day despite the circumstances. Ron was allowed to spend two hours at the church before he was escorted back to the prison. I left the church and returned to the apartment with my roommate Sharon. Our honeymoon and together time came eighteen months later.

I told and retold the deception until Ron came home and became a father to our child and in truth became my husband and provider.

Times were different then. It was unacceptable to be an unwed mother and I was convinced that it was unacceptable to be a pregnant teacher, especially with my pending circumstances, so I resigned from my position. I wasn't ordered to resign though I was advised by an influential person. I regretted following that advice for years to come.

My first major lie was a youthful act to make myself feel more important. My second lie was to protect myself from correction and my third lie was to hide the truth –which at the time was too painful and overwhelming to share.

*****

I was thin during those years so when I became pregnant the weight I gained was not noticeable until late in my term. I was finally at the average weight for my height. So, appearance wise, it was somewhat easy for me to maintain my secret.

The Secret

I drove to 2801 North Gantenbein Ave, to Emanuel Hospital in Portland, Oregon. After parking my car I walked through the hospital doors and took the elevator up to the third floor. It was March 30, 1970. I knew Marilyn's room number so I passed the nurse's receptionist desk. It was during visiting hours so I felt it was acceptable to go directly to her room.

I was a visitor; in five months I would be a patient.

Outside of her door was a clip board hanging on a hook. Her name was on the top line and underneath were the names of her doctorial team: Bolten, Mark, and Neilson. I thought this is a coincidence, I'm seeing Dr. Bolten, too, but I couldn't let Marilyn know, at least not yet.

Marilyn was resting. I tiptoed into the room and laid flowers and a Van Duyn Candy box on the tray next to her bed. Sitting down on the arm lounge chair beside her, I only relaxed a moment when she awoke. "I'm sorry," I muttered, "I didn't mean to wake you."

"Hey Linda, don't worry about it. All I've been doing is sleeping. I'd much rather be awake and visit. Did you bring those flowers and candy?"

"Yeah," I answered.

"You shouldn't have done that. You know you didn't have to do that."

"I know but I thought you deserve something special now that you are a mother."

"Well, I think there's a vase in that cupboard over there if you want to put them in some water." Marilyn was always quick to take care of practical things first.

I answered, "Sure." I got up and found the vase and arranged the flowers in the water. Then we shared the candy.

"Have you seen our baby yet?"

"No, I just came straight to your room."

"Well, I'll call the nurse to help me get my leg on and then we can go see him."

I knew I could have wheeled Marilyn down in the nearby wheelchair, but I also knew Marilyn; she would want to put her leg on rather than use the wheelchair, so I didn't even suggest it.

Marilyn pressed her call button and then we waited.

"Let me tell you Linda, having a baby is awful. I was in labor for twenty hours, with constant wrenching pain. Finally, I said (more like I yelled) I can't take it any longer. That's when they consented to do a C-section. I'm never having another baby. Awful, just awful!"

I wanted to stop Marilyn from telling me these painful details. I didn't want to hear about her long labor. I was thinking, "Tell me something good and positive about having a baby."

Instead, I just had to listen and be sympathetic.

Marilyn went on, "It was excruciating pain. It felt like my insides were being torn out. Now I'm sore from the stitches. It may be weeks before I'll be near normal again. It was just awful, awful, awful."

I thought back to when Marilyn and I were young. We were in fifth grade sitting on the school playground monkey bars. It was there that Marilyn explained to me and to Patsy and Nancy about the birds and the bees. She said she knew all the facts because her brother had explained it all to her.

She was very graphic in her description, not using birds and bees as examples, but talking about the male and the female, their body parts and nudity and the process of how babies begin. I was shocked. I really had not questioned the process of birth before that time and to be given complete details was a picture I didn't want to accept. I decided then and there it wasn't for me. Never was I going to be with a male, never was I going to have a child.

Matter-of-fact, it was as early as third grade that I decided to be a third grade, old-maid school teacher. I was very inspired by my third grade teacher and I also had seen the movie and read the book titled, "Good Morning Miss Dove." It was all about a teacher who never married and devoted her life to her students. That was my goal, to never marry, to have contact with children as my students, not my off-spring.

I thought about what I wanted to say to Marilyn: *I am expecting a child and I wish I could share my excitement with you. I'm happy and scared. Marilyn, I want so badly to share this news. I want to tell you all about the father. I need you to answer all my questions about pregnancy and giving birth and I want us to share this experience of having a baby.*

But right then, I couldn't tell her my thoughts; I just had to be polite and listen to her tell me about her ordeal.

"Tell me, Marilyn, I thought contractions and pain stopped at intervals and then started up again."

"Let me tell you Linda, once you have your first contractions you're in pain constantly, it doesn't stop, and if it did it would only be for a few seconds before the pain would continue. My advice, don't get pregnant!"

I was so tempted to tell her, it's too late I'm already four months pregnant. I couldn't say those words because I wasn't married to my lover and he was in federal prison. I would have to wait to tell Marilyn my secret; it just wasn't the right time.

The nurse came. I stood in the hallway while Marilyn struggled to get her leg on. Then she hobbled down the hallway while holding my arm. It was only a short distance to the nursery room. We looked through the window and saw the bassinet with the name Baby Mark Phillips written on the side of the glass.

There was a precious, healthy looking baby boy. Marilyn was so proud and she looked so radiantly happy. As she stared at her baby, I didn't think she was remembering any pain. I felt tears of joy and sadness well up in my eyes, but I didn't let Marilyn see my emotions, not yet.

*****

Ron served eighteen long months in prison. Then he came home and went to work. During that time, with family help, my main job was to care for my baby.

As new mothers, Marilyn and I shared often, over the phone or during get-togethers, all our concerns and knowledge about being a wife and mother. Mostly our conversations were agreeable, but unfortunately, whatever we disagreed about surged to a major climax.

The Argument

We were having one of our usual phone conversations. We had a lot in common, now that we both had a two-year-old child.

The week before we had spent every day at Marilyn and Norm's beach house in Rockaway, Oregon. Ron and I loved being invited to the beach house. I'm not talking about a small cabin. With the help of a building contractor, Norm and Mr. Landsborough, Marilyn's dad, had built a fabulous 2000 sq. foot home with beach front property.

The windows were floor to ceiling. There was a huge living room, compete with a stone fireplace. The kitchen was big enough for three cooks to prepare a meal at the same time.

On the main floor was a bathroom decorated with a fisherman's theme. The sink and bathtub even had colorful fish painted on the white porcelain. In the hallway was a washer and dryer placed on a raised platform, making it more accessible for Marilyn so she would not have to stoop low getting clothes in and out of the dryer.

There was a bedroom on the main floor and two more private bedrooms and another bathroom upstairs.

The basement was complete with pool table, small kitchenette and a mud room (really a sand room.) There was space by the back door where one could sit on church pews, (a collectable piece of furniture) and brush the grainy sand off feet and shoes.

I loved this beach retreat. I loved the beach. Spending time every year on the Oregon Coast was a regular vacation for my family so being at this nice beach house felt homey and relaxing.

I also liked this place because much of the decor was familiar. Several pictures on the wall were ones from Marilyn's childhood home. For example, the oil painting by C.M. Coolidge of dogs playing cards at a poker table. The other picture I related to was of a mother and child playing on the sandy beach with the ocean as a back drop.

Marilyn and Norm were the perfect hostess and host. They encouraged us to be comfortable and enjoy our stay. We felt at home because we were encouraged to stay for as long as a week and do what they were doing. So we did.

For Ron this actually meant hammering nails, painting walls, or working on the roof with Norm to do some repairs. It meant adding boards where needed and doing a slight remodel or addition to complete the beach house.

I helped Marilyn with food preparation and cleaning up after ourselves and watching our children.

It was early July 1972. We were staying at the beach until July 5th. Over the weekend Marilyn invited another couple, Patty and Richard, and their two-year-old to join us.

It wasn't a problem; there were plenty of adequate rooms. The only conflict came afterwards, not during the weekend.

The guys all went fishing. Norm had his own boat, not a commercial fishing boat, but big enough for three guys to have a good day at the lake and plenty of room to bring back our seafood dinner.

Patty, Marilyn and I were taking the kids to the beach, which was Marilyn's front yard. We were experiencing a day of watching youngsters digging tunnels in the sand, building sand castles near the water, and moving small logs and driftwood from here to there to build their private fort.

Patty and I waded in the ocean. We got our shorts wet as one or two waves rose higher than we expected. The kids too would run into the waves and then, as fast as they could turn, run back the other direction. They were completely soaked from the cold Pacific water. The day was warm and the sun did its job of drying their skin, soaking clothes and wet sandy feet.

Marilyn did not go into the ocean. Not that she didn't want to. It was just too much trouble to remove her leg, trust her crutches, and step into the soft, moist sand. It was doable for her to walk on the beach. Patty and I helped to support her. Then we found a perfect spot of logs to lean against so we placed our beach blanket in front of the logs. She could feel the sand and observe the children playing. Her favorite pastime was to bask in the sun. She tanned beautifully, which I did not. I tried, but ninety-nine percent of the time the result for me was sunburn, complete with blisters. For Marilyn, it was a nice even tan, the envy of most women.

July 4th evening came. I knew the kids would be tired and cranky if we dragged them into town to see fireworks, which didn't even start till 10:30 p.m. So I offered to stay at the beach house and care for the children. I knew I could get them bathed, read them bedtime stories, and have them settled down around 9:00 or 9:30.

The other adults agreed when we talked about the crowd in town, having to park the car a distance from the fireworks viewing area, the loud noise and the bothersome responsibility of keeping three two-year-olds happy while waiting for the sky show of fireworks. They decided this offer of free babysitting sounded great. So they left, including my husband Ron, to go see the show. I really was comfortable with the idea of staying home and watching two-year-olds play until bedtime.

I stayed up late and was alert when everyone came back and shared with me the highlights of seeing the fireworks display.

It wasn't until about two weeks later, while talking to Marilyn on the phone (she was living in McMinnville, Oregon and I was living in Portland) when I discovered that Marilyn was annoyed about some incident at the beach house. She actually criticized me, saying that while Ron and I were at the beach I didn't help enough in the food preparation.

I couldn't believe it! I knew I always helped with clean up. Yes, there were probably a few meals that I let Patty and Marilyn prepare without my help. It seemed at the time that two cooks in the kitchen were all that was needed. I remembered one morning when I didn't help crack the clam shells or clean the clams; I didn't like eating clams and I didn't know how to clean them.

I didn't mind other clean-up jobs and I enjoyed watching the kids more than I desired preparing food. I never felt that confident when it came to cooking and especially not in someone else's kitchen. Trying to please two ladies, who had their own ideas and seemed to be doing fine without my assistance didn't seem necessary at the time.

Marilyn's comments really hurt my feelings. It was like a climax to several troubling phone calls. She called me often to compare notes between her child and mine. It started with baby bed times. She'd ask me how late I had to stay up rocking my baby to sleep. Then she would brag that Mark fell asleep at 9:30 and slept through the night.

There were also disagreements about my style of doing things compared to her style, and my taste in furniture (wooden oak) to her more modern Paul Shatz furniture choices. Of course, Norm's grandfather was Paul Shatz so naturally they would have the best in furniture.

After the beach phone conversation I decided, I don't need this. Instead of looking forward to her calls, our conversations were just stressing me out. I didn't feel that I should have to defend my actions all the time. This last talk and insult to me was enough. I felt it was unjustified and I babbled all my frustrations and defense excuses to

Ron until I came to the conclusion enough is enough. I had no intention of calling Marilyn back and no plan to make peace.

Thankfully, I didn't have to. It was just a matter of hours, when Marilyn called me. She didn't even say hello, she just started with her sincere apology, which sounded genuine until the last sentence.

"I'm really sorry I said those things, Linda. We really liked having you and Ron at the beach house. Gee, the kids played so well together. You were a great help keeping the rooms neat and tidy. It was really nice of you to stay with the kids so we could go and see the fireworks. Forget about helping with the meal preparation. Patty and I really liked working in the kitchen. Gosh she even came with some homemade dishes. Remember the hamburger casserole? It was already made. All we did was stick it in the oven. So I'm sorry for my out-of-line, completely ridiculous comments. Please forgive me."

Of course, I caved in and sighed, "No worry, its ok. We really appreciated you letting us come to the beach. It was loads of fun. We can't wait till we get together again in late August." The August trip had been previously planned.

Marilyn responded, "That will be great. We will definitely be together at the beach house again late this summer."

Then she added the honest comment that explained why she was quick to apologize and to be the first peacemaker when usually I would be the first one trying to settle a disagreement.

"In case you are wondering why I called back so soon - Norm told me to call you immediately. He said our friendship was too important to have a silly argument. He thought you might be really upset about what I said, so he ordered me to call you *now*."

I paused in shock. Here I thought it was totally Marilyn's initiative. I should have known better from years of experience when usually I was first to call to resolve issues. I sighed and said, "Forget it, I'm glad you called. Everything is fine. We can always rise above a slight disagreement." Then I added one last thought, "Tell Norm thanks."

*****

In the year 1974 Ron and I had our second child. In 1978 we had our third child and in 1980 we had our fourth child. During these adult years, Patsy and I lived contrasting lifestyles. By 1980 I was raising four children and babysitting for neighbor families

Differences

During the eighties, Patsy's lifestyle and mine were completely opposite. Patsy was living in a tent in Hawaii. In 1976 Ron was offered a job opportunity in Minnesota so we moved to Minnesota. Patsy was single. I was married. Patsy was not raising children. I was raising my four children and babysitting for neighbor families.

Patsy's concerns were digging holes for water catchments, gathering food, gardening, cooking food over an open campfire, and caring for wild stray cats.

My concerns were to pay the bills, nurse my baby, and get the kids off to school on time. Living in Minnesota required us to hide in the basement during tornado warnings, and to keep our car warm during the winter months by remembering to plug it into a heater or cover it with a blanket whenever we parked it anywhere. The other duties were to keep the snow shoveled so the walkway and driveway would not become a frozen layer of ice.

The extreme seasons of Minnesota, the humidity and mosquitoes, heavy rains, lightning, thunder and summer tornado watches, and six months of below-freezing temperatures kept us busy.

Patsy was able to visit me one time during the nine years I lived in Minnesota. I wasn't able to go to Hawaii so our communication was via (what we now call) snail mail.

Even back then Patsy remarked in one of her letters how different our life paths were:

...Yes, we ended up living pretty different lives from each other, didn't we?

She also wrote about her latest adventures that were completely different from what I was experiencing.

Off and on I've been staying on some land that belongs to a couple named Just and Jym and their baby. I've been hanging around a guy named Sunshine, who lives on the land. Another person, Jasen, also lives there. There is no house. Everyone sleeps outside and I use my tent. It's beautiful land, but needs a lot of work. So when I stay there I work in the morning planting the garden, picking papayas or caretaking of macadamia nut trees. Sunshine and I look alike and people always ask if we're brother and sister.

He's pretty much a fruitarian and is very much into health. I've learned a lot being around him. I'm getting into a more natural way of living, eating fruit right off the tree, working on the land, sleeping outside and oh yes, not wearing clothes. No one wears clothes at Just and Jym's place or at the beach where I go. It's wonderful to feel sun on your whole body. Every one I know is pretty spiritually developed and into health and living a natural life.

I took a trip around the island with Sunshine for about five days. I'm staying on the beach in my tent and fasting for a few days. It's kind of a vacation before I look for another job.

On the trip we stopped at all the natural food stores and co-ops on the island because Sunshine is distributing a new health magazine. We hiked into Waipio Valley, which is an incredibly beautiful valley in the northeast part of the island. We went to Akaka Falls, a beautiful waterfall, and stayed with a friend of Sunshine's who lives there. We all went into Hilo one day and had a big time in the big city visiting the natural food stores, driving around in a rental car and taking people places and returning the car for Leah's friend (Leah is Sunshine's friend who we stayed with.)

Saturday we went to a Health Fair outside of Hilo. There were lectures, people giving massages (free), people selling books, food, and juice. It was great. Ran into a few people I knew. The next day we drove down the east coast where the black-sand beaches are. The highlight of the day was the Queen's Bath, which is a big hole formed in the lava where somehow water gathers (maybe a spring). Back in the old days Hawaiian royalty used to bathe there. We have a small one over here in Kona, but this one was really big and we spent the afternoon swimming.

We camped at Volcano National Park and the next day explored the park. There is a road going all around the Kilauea Crater, which is an active volcano, and various hiking trails off the road. So we did that then returned here Monday night.

We stopped to visit a couple that Sunshine knows, Jay and Joy. Jay is 52 and Joy is 68. They read the Bible a lot and live on a diet that they claim is advocated in the Bible. They only eat fruit and only fruits that readily "yield its seeds." This is fruit that when you open it up seeds can fall to the ground to grow again. They talked a lot about their beliefs and I felt honored that they shared this with me because I don't think they share their thoughts with many people because they're pretty far out.

About the temperature here, during the day it's in the 80's at night it is around 70.

1980

Dear Patsy,

Your living conditions are more luxurious than what I had imagined - even your tent is rather fancy. I guess the two major things I would miss would be a shower and refrigerator - how do you manage to keep food frozen? Here we could do without a refrigerator during the winter, except everything would be frozen.

Well, I've been busy, mostly taking care of children. I think I told you that I'm also babysitting a little girl in the mornings and another neighbor girl that goes to kindergarten in the afternoons. Your mom sent me a letter. She enjoyed her camping experience while visiting you. She also wrote that she can't imagine me with four children (I can't imagine it myself) and she thinks it is "fantastic!" I should frame that statement.

Despite the fussy times I am very thankful for my family. I really enjoy holding my baby Katrina and thinking about what a miracle she is. Babies seem so close to touching a part of heaven.

I got the secretary position I was telling you about for the ladies church group. I already had to write the minutes for the first board meeting. I think I did a lousy job. The first meeting I had to bring Katrina along so the first twenty minutes I was busy feeding her and trying to remember what was said. The rest of the time I was worrying about whether she would cry or not. I don't think I made a very good impression. Next meeting will be Thursday night, so time will tell how well I do at this.

I should do housework - also I have some meat I should put on the stove for our dinner - two things you don't have to worry about. I'll close for now. Glad we are friends despite our differences. Love, Me

P.S. Sometime soon we will have to share our living experiences - you will have to come visit me and maybe sometime I could even visit you. I think I could survive if I had money along so at least one night I could treat myself to a motel room with a shower and get a hamburger sandwich if the urge got real strong.

*****

My marriage to Ron became a troubling relationship. The following story is taken out of chronological order, to explain the blessings and the downfall of this marriage from beginning to end. This chapter tells about when Ron was first released from prison and explains our reasons for moving miles away and our return back to the Northwest.

Late one afternoon Nancy introduced a troubling prediction.

A Walk on the Beach

"How can you tell if a man is true to you or not?" Nancy surprised me with the question. I wasn't sure if she was talking about one of her many boyfriends or if she was asking if I had any doubts about my husband Ron.

We walked on the wet sand close to the ocean waves at Rockaway Beach. Marilyn had invited Nancy and me down to the beach house for a girls' weekend. It was awkward for Marilyn to walk on the beach, yet she graciously encouraged Nancy and me to take a leisurely walk before dinner time.

I told Nancy: "I'm not sure how to tell, but I'm positive Ron is true." Ron and I had been married for six years and we had two children ages six and two. He worked as a shoe sales clerk in Portland. The owner of the store had planned to retire and possibly sell his business. Ron quickly went from shoe clerk to manager and there was hope that within the year he would run the store - with a future of maybe owning the company.

We were comfortable in a new home and meeting all our obligations. I was content being a mother and happy being a wife. I worked part time and was considering two possible full-time teaching offers. One was at a school I had worked at as a long - term sub; they wanted a first grade teacher. The other offer was working as a third grade teacher with the principal being my former college roommate. She called and told me about a job opening. Then she offered me the position and said my oldest child could attend the same school. Our circumstances and life goals looked positive. Ron was great with the children and attentive toward me. I didn't think anything would change.

"Well, Nancy here are some reasons I know Ron is faithful and I trust him completely. Our relationship is very close and we've already been through eighteen tough months of separation when we longed to be with each other every day. So now we appreciate our moments of being together. Our loving is good too - gee we sleep every night in each other's arms. There hasn't been a night that he hasn't been beside me. He likes me for the person I am and accepts me as I am. Not only is there work and raising children, but we have lots of fun together laughing, and you know Ron, he always likes to go and do things so life is not dull. I know he is faithful."

That was how I answered Nancy before my life shattered. My reality was like the song, "Smoke Gets in Your Eyes" The song implies there is "something" that lets you know for sure about your love. It also suggests that the feeling is so powerful there would be no doubt.

This is how I felt before Ron lost his job at the shoe store. The man retired and closed his shop. There was no opportunity of taking over ownership. Ron went into another line of work. He worked for a janitorial company and it involved night work. The owner of this company was a playboy and even though he was married he wanted Ron to participate with him during late nights meeting gals at the bar scene. The excuses Ron would give me were ones that involved having to "work late."

During the next year his actions went from bad to worse. I discovered the truth, yet, I believed in marriage and I vowed to hang on. I prayed and hoped that somehow God would bless our family and heal the brokenness.

So when Ron pleaded for forgiveness and begged me to move with him for a new start and a better paying job in Minnesota I agreed. It would be after nine years of living in Minnesota and after we had four children before I realized that I was married to a man of two personalities. He was the man I admired and loved - a good father, a devoted Christian and a loving husband, but he was also the other man of dishonest character that could change like a chameleon and be off doing his own thing with no regard of consequences.

I came to a conclusion that I could no longer be an honest person and be united with a dishonest person. It was after seventeen years of marriage that I realized that it had ended. I could not immediately walk away, but I knew we would no longer be together.

My family and friends supported me in my decision. Marilyn and Norm were involved at times because Ron was a good friend with Norm and it was disappointing that the four of us could not enjoy fun times anymore.

Ron and I moved back to Washington, but then Ron left for California. I did not follow him. One afternoon I was alone at Redondo Beach in Des Moines, Washington. My kids were visiting their father in California. I walked down the sandy path and sat on the wooden dock. I slipped off my sandals and dangled my legs over the water and felt the cool waves splash my feet. Then I started to hum a tune and added the lyrics using my own version: "Sittin' on the dock of the bay," feeling lonely and sad, listening to the water waves and even my kids are away.

I didn't know then that within the next few years there would be another man in my life. I prayed for another man to be in my life. I asked God for one stipulation that was in the form of one word. At the time I would hear it repeated on the radio frequently from a song by Billy Joel: "Honesty." The song suggests that honesty is very rare but it is also what is needed. It was exactly what I prayed for - an honest man.

*****

During the year 1989 God did give me an honest man. In the year 1990 I married Rod Eddleston. We bought a home in Longview, Washington. In the year 1998 Patsy was staying in a three-bedroom rental house. It seemed like an opportunity for me to visit her and Rod agreed. So in honor of the memory of my mother, who always wanted to go to Hawaii, but was unable to and passed away in 1989, I went to see Patsy.

A Hawaii Visit

Near the shoreline of the Pacific Ocean I saw the small blue church. Black lava rocks surrounded its foundation even though it was situated near the sandy beach.

I told my friend Patsy, "I've seen this church before."

Patsy was puzzled by my remark, "But, you've never been to Hawaii before so how could you have seen this church?"

"It's true I haven't actually been here, but I've seen a photograph of this very same church."

I had to think and remember. Where did I see the photo? Then I recalled. It was years ago in a 1975 set of Britannica Junior Encyclopedias. Under the picture was this caption: "A Roman Catholic Church stands in Kona on Hawaii Island. The first Roman Catholic missionaries came to the islands in 1827."

It is odd, but of all the photos and information in those books this one picture stayed in my memory. It was like a premonition that someday I would actually be at this church.

Patsy and I entered the church through the unlocked doors. There were twelve wooden pews. In front was the altar. The window behind the altar had an etched window pane facing the ocean.
The picture engraved on the glass was Jesus walking on the water. He was reaching for Peter's hand as Peter was leaving the fishing boat on the Sea of Galilee.

Patsy was renting a medium size place, like a mobile home, with three bedrooms in Hilo, Hawaii. During this time her mother was there visiting with her. They shared this roomy place, and welcomed me as a guest too.

I thought seeing Hawaii would be like seeing paradise, as it is often described. Hawaii was like visiting a pleasant, beautiful garden, but one incident happened while I was there which caused me anxiety and worry and marred my visit.

It wasn't anything that I could blame on Hawaii or on my friend Patsy. It was an incident that happened at my home in Longview, Washington and I was too far away to deal with any troubling issues.

As I made my plans, Patsy told me all the details I would need to know about my flying experience. The flight would be from Portland, to San Francisco, to Honolulu. Patsy told me, that once I landed in Honolulu, I was to catch a Wikiki ("a quick" shuttle to the inter-island airport) and then take the next plane to Hilo.

Patsy met me at the Hilo airport and welcomed me to Hawaii by placing an orchid lei around my neck.

I was feeling great. It was a joy to see Patsy. It had been months since we'd been together. After the long flight, I had taken two Excedrin and drank a glass of seven-up at the airport in Honolulu. So now I was minus the headache, which I had been suffering with on the plane, and I was energized.

Before we even left the airport Patsy said, "Before we go to my place I'm taking you to another place to show you that Hawaii can satisfy what you might long for and what you might need while here."

I couldn't imagine what Patsy was referring to and what she thought I might need.

She kept the secret of our destination until we arrived at McDonalds. Patsy is vegetarian yet she knows I like hamburgers. She wanted me to eat the last hamburger I would probably get while in Hawaii. I wasn't even in the mood for a hamburger, but I was pleasantly surprised. She was so thoughtful. She had gone out of her way to prove to me that I could exist in Hawaii, at least for a week.

After we arrived at her place and greeted her mom, Patsy showed me my guest room. It was a room separated from the main house complete with a nice size bedroom and private bath with a shower. It was decorated with bright red, anthuriums and various orchids.

After hours of fun conversation and laughter, I finally got ready to settle down for the night. I was almost asleep when I noticed these black, beetle-like creatures near my suitcase. I dialed Patsy's number on my phone, as she told me to do if I had any problems.

"Yes?" She answered ready to be at my service.

"Sorry to bother you, but there are a couple of guests in my room..."

"Oh, do you see any geckos?"

I looked around and for the first time I noticed an emerald gecko hanging on the ceiling.

I imagined that gecko slithering through my sheets while I slept and decided he would have to go too.

"Yes," I replied, "there is a gecko here, but I called for another reason. There are two huge like beetles crawling near my suitcase."

Patsy responded, "Those are probably cockroaches, they don't like people and usually stay hidden. I will be right over."

She came in wearing her sandal thong shoes and her loose fitting night attire. I was sorry I had to disturb her. She got on her knees to catch the cockroaches. While crawling on the floor, she gave an explanation. "Cockroaches won't harm you, but they are rather creepy creatures and they move very fast."

Then she demonstrated how fast as they slipped though her fingers. She was an expert at this. On her second try, she quickly caught them, in her cupped hands, and threw them out the door.

Next, she climbed on the nearby chair and reached to the ceiling to get the sleepy, lazy gecko. She asked me, "Do you know about geckos?"

I knew they were lizards, but that was about it. This was the first gecko I had met.

Patsy shared a few facts. "Geckos are considered to be good luck tokens and they love eating insects, which is helpful. They are actually friendly and harmless reptiles."

"Reptile" was the key word for me. Friendly, or not, I did not want to worry about his whereabouts during the night.

Patsy gently let it loose in the garden outside the doorway.

"Now rest comfortably," she advised as she left to return to her room.

"Good-night Patsy, it is fun being here and thanks for coming to my rescue."

The next day was our all- day tour of Hilo. Some of downtown Hilo was a park and golf course area because, as Patsy explained, back in 1946 a fifty-six foot tsunami hit Hilo. In the memory of that tragedy and for fear of future occurrences, the land remains undeveloped.

We took pictures in one park by the statue of King Kamehameha. Later, I read more information about King Kamehamehea and discovered there was a series of Kamahmehas from chief Kamehameha to King Kamehameha V.

One afternoon, we hiked around Kahuan Falls and Akaka Falls. Patsy was a tour guide naming all the plants and trees. We had other tourists following us on this trail just so they could hear Patsy's dialogue of information.

One lady asked her, "How long have you lived in Hawaii?"

Patsy answered, "I've been here for nineteen years."

Then she continued to give us detailed information. "The Akaka Falls, off in the distance, are 442 feet. People used to swim and play in these water falls, but now there is too much overgrown vegetation. The other falls are the Kauna Falls. They are 100 feet high."

Our mile hike was like going through a rainforest. The rushing water sounds almost drowned out our voices until we walked along one path area that was surrounded by a jungle of overgrowth ferns and bamboo stems. There we could hear the birds loudly chirping and the water racing into the creeks below.

Patsy continued to point out plants along the way. "Over there are some wild orchids, and notice the Bird of Paradise. Right near our walkway are the hanging Heliconia flowers and the Split Leaf Philodendron."

One lady had been on this moderate hike before and all she wanted to do was hurry on the path. I was glad that I was lingering to enjoy the beauty and I was proud of Patsy for being such a good leader. I was telling myself not to let beauty whiz by me in the future, but to slow down and enjoy the sights. Seeing the sights was all I had to do while in Hawaii.

I didn't have any worries on my mind, until that evening when I received the phone call from my husband. He called to say that our teenage daughter, Katrina, did not come home from the library on time and now it was 11:00 p.m., his time, 8:00 p.m. Hawaii time, and he hadn't heard from her.

I was very concerned because she had been hanging around some other teens that I was not pleased with. There was a fear of drugs and alcohol being a part of her life style. I had yet to catch her with evidence to prove my suspicions, now my inner worries came to the surface.

The evening the phone call came we were at Patsy's place relaxing after dinner and watching a home video comedy. I hated to spoil the fun by explaining to Patsy and to Hazel (her mom) about my phone call. Obviously, they could see I was upset, so I poured out my concerns.

Hazel was a quiet person, but whenever she spoke I felt that she shared words of wisdom. So I listened. She was positive Katrina was safe and would return home. I guess she assumed that Katrina took advantage of the situation of me being out of town and her step-father in charge so she decided it was a choice time to do as she pleased. Coming straight home on a Friday evening was probably not an option she considered.

I felt like a shower of anxiety poured over my head, but I was determined to hang on to Hazel's encouraging words. I was over two-thousand miles from home. There was nothing I could do. If I was home I would be calling on her friends or searching the streets looking for her, but I didn't have all her friends' numbers with me, I could not roam the streets so I depended on my husband and her siblings to do what they could to find her. All I could do was pray and I did. I prayed for her safety and prayed that God would bring my daughter home.

I went to bed that night not worried about geckos or cockroaches, rather worried about my daughter's whereabouts. Not only did I worry, I also felt angry that she would do this when I was having a relaxing time in Hawaii and setting this time aside to honor the memory of my mother.

The next day we continued with our plans. Cell phones were nonexistent then so we had a choice: stay at home all day waiting for a positive phone call, which may or may not come, or go to a place called, "The Millionaire's Pool."

The Millionaire's Pool isn't a sight normally seen by tourists because it is hidden down a long red-dirt road and behind palm trees on the ocean. Here was a pool of salt water, from the ocean, dammed by rocks. In this enclosed area the depth of the pool was only five feet. This was perfect for swimming and that is what Patsy and I did.

Later that afternoon we went to Hawaii Volcano National Park. Madame Pele became a familiar goddess while visiting the volcano area. This place is considered her home. Hawaiians often leave offerings at the volcano area. For tourists there is this rule: "Nothing can be taken except photos, and nothing is to be left behind except footprints."

At the Kilauea Caldera, which is a two- mile crater, steam was coming up from below. This volcano is active and in 1990, eight years before I was there, it erupted and demolished one of the visitor centers and destroyed the fishing village of Kalapana, which included the destruction of 182 homes. Despite how alive and destructive this volcano is, it is still a place active with visitors. It is said that the volcano can erupt, but it is a slow process so people visit these areas and feel somewhat safe while doing so.

The Volcano House, where President Roosevelt hung out years ago, was open for tourists and for lunch guests. We ate there. We also walked through the Thurston Lava Tube. Thurston Tube is like a cave tunnel where molten lava flows underground then cools and forms this tube. Tourists enter one side and leave on the other side.

That evening I got the phone call I was hoping for. "Hello Mom. I'm sorry I was out so late last night. I did come home, but it was early in the morning. I slept all day or I would have called sooner. Rod said I had to call you. I didn't mean to upset you."

Instead of releasing my anger by verbally scolding my daughter, my heart melted with relief of just hearing her voice. I told her Rod and I would hear her explanation (excuses) and discuss the consequences when I arrived home. My heart relaxed and my stomach no longer ached. I was ready to continue my adventures in Hawaii.

The next day Patsy and I did venture. She drove and we traveled from Hilo to Kona. On the way we stopped at the beach that became my favorite beach of all the beach areas we saw (we had visited several.) Hapuna Beach has smooth, soft white sand. We waded in the waves that came in slow and steady. Patsy said that this was the shore line where surfers first learned to surf.

Kona is a town full of souvenir shops. Here is where I bought a glass plate designed with colorful fish. We stayed at the King Kamehameha Hotel and swam that evening in the outdoor pool.

At the end of the week my vacation time was over. It was another wonderful visit with Patsy. For years Patsy had shared with me, via phone calls, letters, and photos her experiences in Hawaii. She had even sent me tapes, and on the tapes I could hear the background sounds of the birds chirping or the frogs croaking on a warm summer night or the background roar of the ocean, now finally, I was able to experience Hawaii.

On this trip, Patsy showed me the sights that I had heard about. We went to a land plot where she once lived for several years. On this land there was no house, she had used a tent for shelter. We toured a boarding house where she stayed for a couple years and we met some people that were still living there. One gentleman thought Patsy and I were sisters. That comment was one that we often received when we were young. Then she drove us (her mom and me) to her newly purchased land where she planned to put a house (not build a house, but move a house) to the property.

At the Hilo airport I hugged Hazel and Patsy. Then I boarded the plane to start my trip back to the mainland. I had experienced the peacefulness and beauty of the island. I enjoyed the companionship of my dear friend Patsy and her mother. I was thankful for my trip to Hawaii. I yelled, "Aloha" which is one word meaning "hello, good-bye and love." It is one parting word that expresses it all.

*****

Marilyn and I came to the conclusion that if we were to see Nancy, we would have to go to California.

California Reunion

Marilyn said she forgave me. I knew immediately what she was talking about. The incident happened eleven years before, but it was always in the back of my mind and probably in the forefront of Marilyn's mind.

In August of 1991, I was celebrating my first wedding anniversary with my second husband, Rod. Marilyn was celebrating her twenty-fifth anniversary with her only husband, Norman. Of course, I was invited to their celebration. Everyone in my family was invited. It happened on the same weekend that my husband planned a get-away for us to celebrate our first anniversary.

Rod and I could have gone to the beach by way of McMinnville, Oregon, where Marilyn and Norm were living, which is what I wanted to do. I tried to persuade my husband that it would be best if we went to this anniversary party first then to our beach resort. I was trying hard to please my man and to please my long time best friend. It seemed impossible to do both. So I reluctantly consented to going to the beach on the more direct route and miss Marilyn's party.

At the time, Rod did not know Marilyn very well, but I knew her. I knew she wasn't going to lightly accept my decision. I didn't realize to what extent she would hold a grudge against my decision.

It was the year 2002 when on the plane to California Marilyn brought up the subject. "I decided to forgive you for not coming to my 25th anniversary party."

I responded, "Really, I thought you forgave me years ago."

"No, I just came to the conclusion last Sunday when I was in church. The message was about forgiveness and I realized I was still mad that you didn't come to the party. I mean, gosh, even your dad, brother and other family members came, but not you. You were my maid of honor. Maids of honor are supposed to come to wedding anniversary celebrations."

From her detailed description of the long ago event I wondered if I really was forgiven or not; certainly the incident was not forgotten. Then she continued.

"Yes, I decided to forgive you."

"Well," I sighed, "I'm glad that you have."

I didn't want to apologize anymore for my grievous infraction. For years I felt sorry that I hadn't been more insistent on going to the party. Rod would have understood if I was firm about the situation. I could not undo the past. So now it was definitely resolved and that was that. We were on our way to visit our friend Nancy and it was good that this past issue got resolved before the plane landed.

Marilyn had concerns about flying even before we boarded the plane. She carried a doctor's statement that she had an artificial leg which might set off the security alarms.

When we checked in I somehow got in the line first. To my surprise, I was asked to empty my entire purse. At the time I had a large purse filled with miscellaneous necessities including a black notebook. It was the notebook that set off the warning signal.

It was embarrassing to dump everything in my purse while people patiently waited for the security guards to sort through my pile.

It became more embarrassing for Marilyn as they escorted her into a private room where she had to remove her shoes and lift her pant leg to prove that she really had an artificial leg. They had taken her purse so she was without her shoe horn and that was needed for her to remove her shoe. So she was distressed with her inability to quickly do the requested task of taking off her shoe. We did make it through these agonizing minutes and got on the plane on time.

The other hassle we experienced was to depart from the plane by climbing down a flight of steps that had been wheeled to the plane. Marilyn was able to do it despite her handicap. I was concerned for her, but when the stewardess asked if it was alright, Marilyn just said yes, she could do it.

In Burbank, California Nancy met us outside the door by the baggage department. She was driving a bright, new-looking, red station wagon.

Even though Nancy never married, or had a family, she lived like a family person would live. She had the car that a person would have when they wanted extra passengers to ride comfortably and she lived in a four-bedroom, two-bath home in Granada Hills, California; I don't mean a small place.

This is how I described her home and her living style: There were two dogs, one cat, self-cleaning litter box, instant hot water (very impressive) remote switches for lamps and fans, hardwood floors, a dressing room, a patio overlooking the golf course, land enough for the dogs to roam, a built-in barbecue, grapefruit trees, a brick mailbox, perfectly paved circular driveway, a quiet, lovely neighborhood, dining room, family room, living room and sunny days. Who could ask for more?

She said she got a wonderful deal on this house because she purchased it in 1995 one year after the severe Northridge Quake near LA. No one wanted to buy a home in Granada Hills near where the earthquake had done extensive damage.

Nancy's dogs and her cat were there to greet us. Marilyn made a comment about when her first son, Mark, was born they had a puppy. She went on to say, "The puppy was hard to handle and the baby was crying and Norman said," 'When I get home from work either the baby or the puppy has to go.' Marilyn added, "That was the end of the dog."

I jokingly asked, "Are you sure you made the right choice?"

I thought to myself, knowing Norman I knew he was not serious, but it was good that it wasn't me who made that choice - I would have wanted baby and puppy. Matter-of-fact, when my second child was born my dog had four puppies just a few weeks before I gave birth.

The first evening we went out to eat at an Italian Restaurant. Then we went grocery shopping. We had not been grocery shopping together, ever, so this was an experience that certainly demonstrated our differences in taste. The three of us could not agree on a cereal choice, a type of bread for toast or what juice to buy. It was amazing. We had been friends for years but never lived together and now we were discovering that on some basic issues, like foods, we had nothing in common. We finally settled on something for the next day's breakfast at least, though some of our morning was eating fruit right off the grapefruit and orange trees in Nancy's yard.

That evening we spent hours talking, laughing and sharing deep emotions of our lives. Even answering personal questions that maybe we never asked before. We retold stories of our childhood and teen years. Marilyn shared feelings about the time, when she was fifteen and had her major accident. She recalled when she was in the hospital for three months and in a body cast for the whole summer. Now, when she looked back on the situation she didn't think she would be able to endure as she did then. We came to the conclusion that God gives us strength during the moment of our need.

The next day was all day at Disneyland. Disneyland is like visiting another world. It is a place on earth where imagination comes alive. Childhood characters from storybooks and movies are real.

Adults and children dance on the streets and bands and parades happen frequently. Costumes are acceptable street-wear and people, even babies and children, are happy and smiling.

The streets sound like a school playground of children laughing and having fun mixed with the sounds of talking adults, and often background music. There is a variety of foods offered so the smells of caramel popcorn, hot dogs and other cultural foods are mixed together, tempting us to stop and taste.

Marilyn and Nancy were daring and willing to ride all the rides. I hesitated and selected the rides I wanted to ride on. I was experiencing my, on rare occasions, claustrophobic feelings. I didn't want to go on any ride where I felt enclosed, upside down or had to wear a seatbelt that automatically latched and unlatched. I knew it was silly of me to have these apprehensions on my mind, but it was the way I was feeling.

Marilyn didn't understand my phobia dilemma. It was a physical effort for her to even be in California let alone go on rides in Disneyland and she thought I was missing the opportunity of enjoying our time to the utmost. I ignored some of her sarcastic comments, like, "I suppose Linda will only want to ride on the kiddy roller coaster."

Really, Marilyn and Nancy rode on the kid's roller coaster. I did not, but I did ride on several other rides and my favorite was the "Indiana Jones Adventure," even more daring than the small roller coaster. For this ride we rode in an open army jeep and luckily I got the steering wheel seat. I felt like I was in control, though really I had no control. The jeep was moving on roller coaster rails flying by cobra eyes, flashing lightning, and flaming lava Then we quickly descended down dark, narrow, steep cliffs; very thrilling, but not a claustrophobic experience.

The following day was a guided tour with Nancy as our guide. It was see all you can see in one day. She drove her car through LA traffic like a pro. We went to Malibu, Sunset Blvd., the University of California, Bel Air, and Beverly Hills. In Beverly Hills, Nancy pointed at homes of the rich and famous and the Beverly Hills Hotel.

We went to see Hughes Laboratory. This is the place where Nancy worked for three years. It is heavily guarded and we were told we could drive through the gated parking lot to see the buildings, but not stop. This was the start of her working for aerospace and what began her lifetime career. She said the only reason she qualified for a prestigious position, working under the Vice President for one of the aerospace companies, in a secretarial position, was because she knew shorthand. She took shorthand in high school against her high school counselor's advice. The reasoning was Nancy wasn't doing well in biology so the counselor didn't think she would do well at Short Hand. From that negative advice, Nancy accepted it as a challenge and got straight A's. That was her entrance to a job career.

Hollywood was our next quick tour. I asked to stop long enough to see the Sidewalk of Stars. Nancy was on a roll of "Let's keep seeing the sights," however, she stopped long enough for me to have a few moments on the sidewalk. I jumped out of the backseat. She drove the car around a few blocks then honked her car horn allowing me enough time to jump back in the backseat. I saw the golden stars on the black marble of Hank Williams and Marlene Dietrick. I was wishing I had more time to list all the names and learn more about each famous person.

We drove past Hollywood High. I yelled out, "That's where Rod graduated from."

Later, Marilyn pointed out The Mormon Temple, the second largest Mormon temple, the only larger one being in Utah. Looking upward we could see the statue of the angel Morori on top of the temple steeple.

That evening Nancy fixed us dinner and we watched the movie, "Family Man."

The next day was a tour of Chinatown and the Mexican Bazaar. We threw our pennies in a wishing well. I've always thought about my friends when I've heard the song, "Three Coins in a Fountain." I've wondered over the years if we got exactly what we wished for, or did we get pleasant surprises, or extreme disappointments. Would we have wished differently, and what did we wish for now?

This visit to California was a joyous reunion of my three friends. It proved that friendship endures the test of time, differences and distance.

*****

I was content being married to my second husband Rod, but we faced several major challenges. My youngest daughter was duel-diagnosed as being bi-polar and drug addicted. In the year 2011 at the age of thirty while living in Brooklyn, New York she died. This news was painful and unbearable.

At the same time, Rod was wheelchair bound from his disease of muscular dystrophy. We were coping despite these harsh circumstances. Yet, we had one more challenge to face. That challenge would prove that we no longer knew how to cope.

A Sunny Day

I took a long driftwood stick and I printed letters in the sand, "Pasty and Linda were here."

Patsy and I were walking along the sandy beach. My husband, Rod, was there too, but not right on the damp sandy shore. He was about fifty feet away on the mile-long paved walkway waiting for us in his power Quantum 6000 candy apple red wheelchair.

We were at Willow Grove Beach, in Longview, Washington overlooking the Columbia River. It was a sunny but cool day in October, 2012.

There is always a peacefulness near the water. The stability of seeing the tide repeatedly reach the shoreline is comforting. The beach was semi-quiet with only the splashing sound of waves hitting the shoreline and a dog barking in the distance. I took deep breaths of the sea air and this helped to relieve my anxious concerns.

Rod and I were going through a crisis. He was not well. Something was majorly wrong and it had nothing to do with muscular dystrophy; the disease that had already made his muscles so weak he could not walk or stand.

Earlier, that same morning, Rod had to go through a CAT scan to determine what made him nauseated all the time and caused him discomfort, especially through the night.

It wasn't our first crisis. Eighteen months before, on April 7, 2011, seven days after she had completed a wonderful visit with all of her family here in Longview and in Seattle and then returned to New York, my daughter, Katrina at the age of thirty, had died.

While Patsy and I waited in the doctor's office for Rod's CAT scan procedure, I shared with her my daughter's poetry and the book I had written about Katrina.

Patsy was in Hawaii when I got the sad news about my daughter. Patsy was involved with a care-giving position and unable to leave. So my friendship support came from a distance. Now she was here and I was so glad. Rod, too, was overjoyed to see her.

We left the doctor's office and the sun was shining. I did not want Rod to dwell on his ills or fears of what prognosis or other future tests he had to face, so I suggested, "Let's go to Willow Grove."

When Patsy and I got back on the paved walkway beside Rod, two incidents happened at Willow Grove to make for a memorable day.

Men were flying overhead in these kite type parachute machines. For thirty minutes we were entertained with the excitement of observing these bodies and machines drifting back and forth in the sky. For this period of time we did not worry about ourselves, rather the concern was the safe landing of these daring souls who trusted these machines to hold them in the air.

Also, a family came by with their dog. The dog came close and sat by Rod. Then he ran off. Within my hearing only, the lady told me that her dog was sensitive to other's pain. Then she added quietly it must not be too bad because the dog didn't stay by Rod too long. In reality, Rod would have less than two more months to live and a cancerous liver tumor would take over and defeat him.

On this day, we had a close friend with us who was telling us to smile as she took photos. Her friendship let us know someone else cared and was concerned about what we were doing and how we were feeling. The two of us strolled and Rod wheeled through the paths of Willow Grove on a sunny day in October.

*****

The opportunity came to attend a Music Teacher's Conference in Southern California. I went and included a visit with Nancy.

California Visit – March, 2013

Nancy told me that before she came to greet me in California she had whispered a prayer. She prayed that God would protect her on the road and protect those around her. She did not know how significant and necessary that request would be.

Nancy and I hadn't seen one another since 2007, six years before. That year we attended Nancy's mother's funeral service in Portland, Oregon. Since then, our communication consisted of e-mails and phone calls.

I knew she was busy maintaining her four bedroom luxury home. I knew that two of her beloved pet dogs had died and that she replaced those painful losses with an adopted puppy named Murfee. His energetic antics renewed her spirit and love for the animal world.

I was aware of her concern for a dear friend whose father was suffering and near death. I had no idea that Nancy was driving a bright new blue PT cruiser with heated car seats. Nor had I realized that she was taking a hiatus from church and church politics to quietly renew and revitalize her relationship to God. I was surprised when she said she still had contact with a male friend who lives in Florida. He being in Florida and her being in California kept them from ever enhancing their friendship to a serious relationship. She was communicating with him years ago when I visited before in California.

She knew about my past experiences. She knew I was still in grief over my daughter's death in 2011 and my husband's death in 2012.

I shared a family collection of photos to give her a recent update. She told me she was sorting through her belongings and was missing pictures from her childhood days. I promised her I would send her some pictures that I'd collected over the years and then we would know which matching pictures we had or which ones we needed to exchange.

Our adventure for this meeting began at four-thirty in the late afternoon with her meeting me right in front of the Disneyland Hotel. She had a restaurant in mind so we headed in that direction.

This pathway became a rollercoaster for me and I am not talking about a ride at Disneyland, rather about facing vivid painful memories.

We were on the freeway with probably less than average amount of traffic. Nancy was somewhat confused as to which lane she was supposed to be in so we were traveling a medium speed, not over the speed limit, when a motorcycle directly ahead of us started to swerve on his bike. It was swaying back and forth as if he was undecided which lane he was going to be in. All of a sudden, at a speed between forty and fifty miles per hour, his bike just flopped on the ground sideways. The rider slid on the pavement right in front of us. He was sliding on his lower back, bottom and the back of his legs.

Nancy stopped immediately and within five feet or less of Nancy's PT Cruiser his body slid in front of us till he landed beside the cement barrier on the side of the freeway. His bike also slid across the pavement, fortunately not in the same direct path as the rider. As it streaked across the pavement the machine appeared smashed and twisted.

Nancy and I reacted the same, and at the exact moment, she yelled out loud "Dear God, oh Dear God" and I was saying, "Please Jesus." These were words not using God's name in vain, but a deep, unified prayer request that this young man, lying on the ground before us would be okay.

Within seconds, this young guy with his helmet still on, his heavy pants torn, and his leather jacket still intact, stood upright and signaled to us with a hand wave that he was going to make it. He walked to his broken bike and took out his cell phone. We were amazed. Four other cars safely stopped and other men were running to his assistance. It was unbelievable. I told Nancy, "We just witnessed a miracle."

We continued on our quest and arrived at Mime's Restaurant. Just as we parked the car I realized that Mime's was a restaurant where my daughter Katrina worked at in Arizona for a while. The memories of the place that appeared like the one in Arizona with similar architecture and decorative flower pots by the entrance penetrated my mind. I felt sad knowing my daughter no longer worked in Arizona, instead, she was buried in New York.

Tears started to form as I reflected on my dear daughter Katrina and remembered our visit in Arizona.

The motorcycle accident we had just witnessed also still consumed my mind. This man was injured, but safe. He could have died right in front of us.

My daughter, Danita, was in a serious motorcycle accident exactly two weeks after my daughter Katrina died. That accident could have taken her life, but by a miracle she was able to recover from her injuries. Seeing a body slide on the pavement and knowing that my daughter at that exact moment was working for the Kawasaki Company doing a show in Florida - and she was probably riding a motorcycle - caused me to relive the haunting memories of her previous crash. This set a gamut of emotions through my mind.

Then I thought about Rod, my husband, who just recently died. If he were alive I'd be telling him about our experience and all the details about Nancy's fancy car.

I took a deep slow breath. Then I continued to smile, chat, and laugh with Nancy. This wasn't the time or place to let my heart reveal how sad I felt. This was a reunion time of being with my best friend. So we jabbered about the past and the present. Our friendship conversations always began wherever we had left off as if there had been no time or distance between us.

I mentioned, "Come to Oregon and we will spend a weekend at Marilyn's beach house." I didn't get a future commitment from Nancy. We ate dinner together, toured the Grand Disneyland Hotel, where she had stayed once, and the Adventure Hotel where I was staying. We went up and down the streets of Disneyland Downtown and listened to music concerts and bought souvenirs. Then we took photos of each other and asked a waitress to take a picture of us together.

Nancy shared some insight about the past and how thankful she was to me for the help my family gave her when she was young. She talked about how she felt about our friendship as kids when the three of us, Marilyn, Nancy and I competed for each other's attention. Then we hugged and parted without a future date of getting together. That departure was rather too quick. I was left with a lingering smile, but also a touch of reminiscence and sadness due to distance and separation.

*****

Still grieving the loss of my husband I decided to help heal my aching heart by visiting my friend Patsy in Hawaii.

Patsy and Hawaii

Patsy is a "kama'aina" (a resident of many years - meaning a child of the land.) In 1978 she, her mother and sister took a vacation in Hawaii. During that visit Patsy fell in love with the spacious land, the friendly people and the mild climate.

In 1979, by herself, she returned to Hawaii bringing with her only one suitcase and limited funds. She purchased a car (the first one being a "lemon" and one that had to be returned) and then she bought a van and toured the big island. She searched for work, a place to stay and a future home. Often she slept in her van during this hippy lifestyle time.

Near Kona she was granted permission to stay on a piece of land in a tent in exchange for helping the land owner with his crop of Macadamia nut trees. Later she agreed to a joint ownership of land with four other people. With a boyfriend named Mike she lived in a huge tent braced above ground to keep out the insects. They covered the tent with an extra tarp to keep out the rain.

Later they built the frame for a house; unfortunately as the house frame went up the relationship deteriorated. Patsy left Mike. Then years later she bought an acre of property outside of Hilo. She found a house in Hilo that had to be moved and then restructured to make a comfortable, livable home. This house looks like a southern plantation place. It has three bedrooms, one bath, kitchen and an enclosed front porch with a covered deck in the back.

In 1999 Patsy wrote this letter to me about the house she was placing on her property:

I'm excited about getting this house. Today it's being tented for termites. Termites are a bad problem in Hawaii. I'm house-sitting across the street from my lot and it looks like the house will

*probably be moved on Sunday. That's good timing-very conve-
nient for me. After it's moved, the next step will be to build the
foundation underneath.*

*I like the idea of getting a recycled house, and it's so much cheap-
er and easier than building a new one. But it still will need a lot
of work. Of course, there's no water supply or sewers out here.
So I will need to dig a cesspool and put up a water catchment. I
had to have more bulldozing done to make a large enough access
to move the house in.*

*Now I have a much bigger cleared area than before and am look-
ing forward to planting trees and having a garden. I have already
planted four fruit trees, a fig, avocado, lime, and mango. I already have a papaya tree that's producing papayas. Also, I have a
pick up truck so I can haul stuff out there.*

*I'm sorry I've been so bad about writing. Maybe when I move
into my house and get a table to write on I will sit down and write
more.*

Love, Pat

*****

It wasn't until 2014 that I was able to see her home in Hilo.

Second Trip to Hawaii

"I can only play in the key of C and G," lamented Patsy.

"Well," I responded, "I can only play the songs that are in this book (a song book published in 1957 that included piano notes and bass chords) so our "concert" is going to be limited. I also think we should skip the Christmas tunes since it is the end of March and we are in the midst of spring time in Hawaii - no way does it seem like Christmas here and now."

"So, 1, 2..." I started to count for the folk song chorus, "O Susanna, don't you cry for me. I've come from Alabama with a banjo on my knee." Pasty played her Casio keyboard and I played her twelve bass accordion that she had on the top shelf in the closet. We were in her guest room in Hawaii and I was the guest.

Three days earlier, March 25, 2014, I left my home in Longview, Washington at 4:30 a.m. to catch a flight from Portland to San Francisco. Then on United Airlines I flew from San Francisco to Honolulu. At 1:55 p.m. (Hawaiian time) Patsy greeted me in Honolulu with a white purple orchid lei. We boarded a shuttle bus to our reserved hotel room at Aqua Palms in Waikiki (the word meaning spouting waters.) Waikiki is a busy neighborhood of Honolulu with tall buildings and a breath-taking beach. Like Manhattan, New York, Waikiki is considered the "city" that never sleeps.

During our first evening it was warm with a slight breeze. People were walking along the white sandy beach and there were several open courtyard restaurants and parks where live music was playing. Hanging fire-lit torches gave brightness to the paved walkways.

From where we walked on the beach we saw Diamond Head. It looked like a huge green grassy mountain. It is a volcanic crater with a view point at its top peak. We also viewed tall buildings across the bay lit with night lights.

On the second floor of our hotel was a rooftop pool. The second morning I went swimming. The pool water was cool and only four feet deep and minus any other person except for me. Patsy is spoiled and she did not want to swim in a shallow cold pool. She wanted to wait and swim in the warm, deep, limitless Pacific Ocean. The next day we spent on the beach and Patsy did swim out in the ocean like a mermaid. I waded in the surf.

In the afternoon on a chartered bus we went to the Polynesian Cultural Center. It was an hour trip to our destination. On the bus our guide referred to us as "cousins" and when we had to wait for two people at one hotel stop he said we had to wait for our "family members." He told us that the word aloha had three meanings depending on how you accented the syllables. Aloha means hello. Accenting the "ha" sound in a sexy tone, means "I love you." Lingering on the o sound of Aloha means good-bye, but also means longing for you to stay or hoping to see you again soon.

On this trip we viewed rural O'ahu. We saw several small towns and rustic- looking schools and businesses with green mountains on one side in the background and the ocean on the other side. We rode on a two-lane paved highway that the driver said was the only road that went around the island.

The Polynesian Cultural Center has forty-two acres of property. We were introduced to our guide and she led us and our group through the activities. Our first show was a parade of canoes and dancers wearing costumes representing their countries. The performers were from: Tonga, Hawaii, New Zealand, Samoa, Tahiti, Rapa Nui and Fiji. These seven islands were represented throughout the cultural center.

We watched a strong, handsome native climb the coconut tree and demonstrate how to crack the coconut. Even though the explanation seemed doable; my suggestion would be to ask a guy like the one climbing the tree to crack the coconut with his machete.

During a New Zealand ceremony we were the visiting tribe meeting the chief of the home tribe. We had to greet the head chief through a ceremonial ritual and give a gift and receive a gift. Then we watched dances that welcomed us as accepted guests.

During one musical show we enjoyed huge ice cream sundaes. Performers and audience participants tried to outdo each other hammering on drums and wildly dancing.

We saw a film that gave us a virtual feeling of flying over Hawaii and seeing parts that are not even accessible to the tourists. It was a powerful feeling of seeing the beauty of nature's wonders, hearing the Hawaiian music and sensing the wonder of this remote creation.

That evening our dinner was a formal Luau. It was an outdoor setting. Over two-hundred people were served this Hawaiian feast. They passed in front of us the roasted Kalua pig. While we ate our Hawaiian dishes hula dancers performed near our tables.

Our final drama presentation told a native story of Hawaii called "The Breath of Life" complete with fire dancing. The message in all of these experiences was their use, love, protection and respect of their lands and their oneness with nature.

The next day we flew to Hilo, where Patsy lives. A Japanese Hawaiian friend of Patsy's named George was waiting for us at the airport. We went out to eat at a Chinese restaurant. Afterwards we went to George's house to get Patsy's car where she had left it while we were in Honolulu. Then we had to drive over dark country roads to another friend's house to get Patsy's dog, Trixie.

It was several years ago that Patsy adopted this pet from the Humane Society. It was a challenge because Trixie was scared of everything beginning with being too fearful to even walk out of the Humane Society doors. Patsy had to carry her until her new pet got use to walking with her. Patsy spent long hours and several months training this special dog. She advised me to take time getting acquainted with Trixie. I did take my time and the dog did too. It wasn't until the end of the week and the end of my stay that Trixie came near me. The rest of the time she kept her distance, staring at me, but not getting too close.

When we arrived at Patsy's home in the dark the first amazing sight we saw was the numerous bright stars that I never see so brightly in the city. I also heard the coqui frogs. I did not see these small frogs, but they made their sounds loud and clear. Patsy told me they make their noises all night long. I slept through the noise.

I also met Patsy's cat named Egypt. She is a black cat and she met us with complaints. She was probably unhappy because Patsy had been away for several days and Egypt had to depend on the neighbors to feed her.

Hilo is a tropical rainforest. I read in one of their papers that the weather forecasts for the months of August through November were listed as a high of 77 degrees and a low of 64 degrees every day. Though the temperatures are always mild they do have rain. Patsy has a tin roof so there were times when we had heavy downpours and I stood on her back porch listening to the steady stream of water flow and the tapping of the drops on the roof.

After staying at her home for a couple days we then toured around the big island of Hawaii. Our first stop was Hapuna Beach. This was my favorite beach when I was in Hawaii back in 1998. The beach was still the perfect spot. We went into the ocean and enjoyed the sandy shore until it started to rain. Then we ate our lunch under a covered picnic area.

The next stop of our journey was Kona. Kona seemed less busy than it was back in 1998. It may have been because it was a rainy week, but also they have problems of "vog haze" it comes from the volcano and can cause breathing problems. It was the reason Patsy did not stay in Kona. It varies from how the wind blows and what the volcano is doing, but it was mentioned by store owners as the reason why fewer people were living or staying in Kona.

It was in Kona that we spent the night. The next morning we attended the oldest Christian church on the island, Mokuaikaua Church. It was founded in 1820. People were dressed nicely, many women wearing skirts or dresses, but everyone was wearing sandals.

We also visited another Catholic church called St. Benedict's Painted Church. Inside this church were wall to ceiling paintings depicting Bible stories or Bible themes.

As we drove along the coast to Kealakekua we stopped and toured the Greenwell Coffee Plantation that my cousin's daughter and husband own. I was unable to see my cousin's daughter, but we toured the grounds and tasted the different flavors of coffee. On our drive back we saw places that were not covered with white sand, or brown land nor green grass, but land covered with thick black lava that appeared to go on and on for miles.

There are five volcano mountains on the big island of Hawaii. They are Kohala, Mauna Kea, Hualalai, Mauna Loa and Kilauea. Of these mountains Hualalai, Mauna Loa, and Kilauea are still considered active volcanoes.

After we returned to Hilo and on the next day, we visited the Hilo Zoo and the Imiloa Museum. It was while we were at the museum that Chile had a severe earthquake (7.0). So that evening we had the fear of tsunami warnings. We did listen to the radio announcements, but mostly we stayed up late to catch up on our memories through retelling, updating and looking through photo boxes that Patsy had saved over the years.

The spirit I captured on this trip was the love of Hawaii. I realized more fully why Patsy longed to live here rather than her hometown Portland. She lived amongst the people; she cared for the land, and became united with the Hawaiian history. Hawaii becomes more than a place to live, but an identity of belonging, a part of the spiritual surroundings and a connection with nature.

At the Hilo airport when it was time for me to leave I said aloha to Patsy with a lingering accent and a sense of sadness. Once again we would be separated by distance. I took a deep breath as I waved good-bye and yelled a grateful mahalo for her hospitality. And she yelled aloha and mahalo back.

*****

This last story is to remember my other best friend, of twenty two years, my late husband Rod Eddleston, to whom I have dedicated this book.

An Honest Man

As I think back to the year 1970, I remember that Marilyn expressed disappointment that I did not invite her to my first wedding. In 1966 I was maid of honor at her wedding. In reality there were no invitations sent to attend my first wedding. I had to get permission from a warden to be married and my groom was escorted with guards standing beside him and then escorted back to prison after the ceremony.

My second wedding (twenty years later) was much different. Marilyn, her husband Norm, and her family were invited to this formal occasion along with about one hundred and fifty other guests. My four children ranging in ages 10 to 19, and Rod's daughter were in the wedding party.

One daughter played the violin, another daughter sang. We also had guitar player/singer, piano, organ and a flute player. There was no music at my first wedding. I wished afterwards I would have provided it even if I had to play a tune myself.

After the pastor announced that we were officially married, and introduced us as Rod and Linda Eddleston, the audience clapped. I felt so honored that in this marriage people expressed their approval. It was a welcomed acceptance. At another location, other than the church, there was a reception of food, fellowship and dancing.

Unlike my first marriage, where our honeymoon was a beach trip eighteen months after we were married, and after my first child was born, for this second marriage there was an immediate honeymoon trip to Canada.

We came back home to a newly purchased house with the responsibility of still raising three children. Rod was a confirmed bachelor with previous girlfriends - one that gave him a daughter. He had no experience living with a wife or kids. The family concept was new to him.

196

There were adjustments we had to make. I noticed certain idiosyncrasies that had to be addressed during the first few weeks of living together. He parked his gray two-door Toyota in the middle of the driveway not once giving a thought that my station wagon belonged there too. His clothes took up the entire double-door closet space in our bedroom. I wondered does he even know I also live here.

Sharing was a new concept for him. After one evening of me writing my feelings and expressing anger over the issue it somehow got resolved, except for the television remote that he never shared when he was home.

Adding more expenses to his life was a challenge too. He was flabbergasted at how much hair conditioner my daughters, each with long hair, and I used over the months. We resolved that dilemma- not by requesting that the girls use less - that was not even an option - rather, we started buying it by the gallon from Costco.

These were minor frustrations. Major episodes happened during our marriage that were not curable. In her late teens my youngest daughter was duel diagnosed as bi-polar and drug addicted. Rod had muscular dystrophy since he was sixteen. These two major diseases did not leave us alone, and like monsters lurked in the room. They were handicaps that could have destroyed our relationship. Instead, Rod and I held firm. We had a rock solid marriage that wasn't going to falter because of circumstances that were beyond our control. We held fast to each other and worked as a team to do the best we could do to conquer each battle one at a time.

We were married for twenty-two years. During those years there was never a doubt or question about his faithfulness. He was an honest, hard worker. He completed a thirty-year career as a social worker and supervisor for the DSHS (Department of Social and Health Services.)

Muscular dystrophy slowed us down at times, limiting certain activities, but we did take trips. We also went to social gatherings and often had parties enjoying fellowship with others.

The first special occasion was our wedding. Rod and I danced together. He held me with his arms around my waist. He was unable to raise his arm up high to hold my hand in a common dance pose, so I too held my arms around his waist. I wore a long flowing light pink and white satin dress. Rod was in a light blue tuxedo. We swayed around the room in what seemed like perfect rhythm. We were dancing to the live band music, led by our friend (Patsy's brother, Ron Walker.) Ron played with his band partner, Elvis' hit song: "Can't Help Falling in Love with You." It was the first song that Rod and I danced to when we started dating. He knew how to dance.

Another fun time was a Halloween party at our house with friends and family. All the adults came in costume, from Robin Hood to the good and bad fairies, the hen pecked husband, the painter, a football player, the beatniks, and we placed a purple wig on my sister. All the grandkids came in costume too. Then, during the middle of the party Rod came out wearing a black leather jacket and an Afro wig. He was Elvis Presley. I always said he had a voice like Elvis's. He played the part well and started talking about how sorry he was for the wrong he did for Priscilla's love. Then with a Karaoke tape he sang "Love Me Tender." Of course, his fans screamed and clapped and expressed their appreciation.

We took a wonderful road trip to California where he was reunited with his family that he hadn't seen for more than thirty years. His nephew located us and invited us to come to Rod's sister's fiftieth surprise birthday party. So we went. He greeted his sister with a loving surprise.

They knew each other as kids, but after Rod's mother was tragically killed in a lightning storm, and then years later his step-father remarried and Rod was sent to live with his biological father, it meant a separation from his two sisters. This reunion opened a door of several trips back and forth. It was a significant time of reuniting his family.

Muscular dystrophy almost whipped us during the last two years of his life when he wasn't able to walk or stand due to his weakness. Yet, even then we adjusted. We functioned with the aide of a fancy power wheelchair, an accessible van, and a Hoyer Lift. Then during the last year of his life we also depended on morning care-giving help.

The last battles were when my youngest daughter at the age of thirty took her own life with an overdose of pills and then the following year Rod was diagnosed with liver cancer and the prognosis of only 2 to 3 months to live. These were the challenges we could not conqueror. He died within the two months.

Before he died he and Marilyn had a phone conversation. Marilyn, too, has suffered over the years with struggles to walk and maintain her body strength after the tragic accident of her youth. She reassured Rod that she believed in heaven. She comforted him by encouraging him with her words of faith. She told him she believed that in heaven there will be no pain and our bodies will be made whole. I trust this conversation helped to reassure Rod.

Despite our challenges, I am happy for those twenty-two years. Rod was my strength. He was weak in physical stamina yet, he was strong in character. I relied on his wisdom and courage to conquer whatever life handed to us. He was my lover, my friend, my husband, and a worthy step-father to my children. God gave me the honest man I needed.

******

These friendship stories end; but the friendships continue. Marilyn, Patsy, and Nancy have read these stories and gave their approval for me to share these memories.

Marilyn and Linda, age 5 - 1950

Marilyn and Norman, age 8 - 1950

Marilyn and Linda at Marilyn's house.
Sabin School in the background - January 1954

Patsy and Linda with their dolls - 1956

Nancy - 1955   *Marilyn - 1955*

Linda - 1955

Linda and Nancy in Linda's backyard - August 1959

Marilyn, Linda and Nancy standing by the Peter Iredale Ship in Warrenton, Oregon - 1959

Patsy - 1962

Nancy - 1963

Linda - 1963

Marilyn - 1963

205

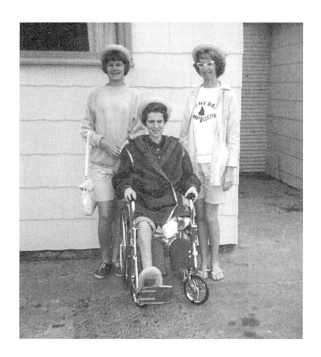

Nancy, Marilyn,
Linda,
Seaside, Oregon
in front of the York
Cabins - August 1961

At Tigre Saying good-bye to Amado and his wife.
Nancy in Peru 1977

Patsy - tent home in Hawaii
Papayas in buckets so birds don't eat them - 1980

Nancy, Marilyn, Linda - 1998

Linda and Patsy in Kona, Hawaii - 2014

Patsy and Linda at Willow Grove, Washington - along the Columbia River 2015.

POST NOTES

The Tangled Mess

Once again I read about a string phone experiment in a book titled, "Science Around the House" by Roz Folcher, copyright 2010. I followed the instructions with my grandson. It was not successful. Maybe our string holes were too large or my paper cups were foam cups or our string was not pulled taut; whatever the reasons we gave up.

In the year 2012, I purchased a used book from the library dated 1930 called, "Facts and Fancies". I was surprised to discover a chapter titled, "How to Make a Telephone". These directions were similar, but more complicated. In this book these items were listed: "an old kid leather glove, two small wooden boxes, a piece of sandpaper, a few small tacks, a piece of paraffin, and a ball of hard cord."

There is a long explanation of how to make a telephone: "Saw off the ends of both boxes. Smooth the edges with sandpaper. Cut two squares from the wrist of the kid glove. These squares should be the size of the end of the boxes. Soak the squares in water for a few minutes."

The directions continue saying to use "the leather while it is wet and stretch it over the box ends and then tack that leather onto the boxes." The directions also suggest coating both leather ends with melted paraffin. Melting paraffin was how my mother burnt our kitchen once when she was making jam so I suggest being extra careful with this step or don't even try this experiment.

The next step listed is to make small holes in the boxes and run the string through and knot the end. Then stretch the string tight. "Do not let the string touch anything." The last sentence of these instructions is: "Then one person can hold the receiver and talk while the other one listens." Despite their complicated directions they make the result sound easy.

At the Cowlitz Fair, in July 2014, they had two cans tied together with a heavy white string. Another child and I each held one of these cans and pulled the string tightly between us and walked a distance from each other. I was excited anticipating the result. Would I hear his voice or only a whisper or silence? Then the child spoke into his can with a normal voice volume. I heard his voice loud and clear by holding my can to my ear. The process works!

It made me wonder if it would have worked between Marilyn's house and my house years ago. Instead, now I will use my land phone, cell phone, and e-mail to communicate with my friend. I used two of these methods recently to talk to Marilyn, not from down the street, rather from across the state line.

The Unwelcomed Greeting

Though Patsy and I disagreed about other subjects, we never argued like we did on the first day we met.

During our pre-teen and teen years we often extended our phone conversations by lingering with long good-byes. We said good-bye in several languages: Pig Latin, Spanish, Japanese, German, Hebrew, French and whatever other way we knew or could imagine. Patsy was good with pronouncing these expressions and I enjoyed learning these new words.

September, 2008

Dear Patsy,

Thanks for your lasting friendship. Over the years you listened to me no matter what words or shocking news I threw at you.

The other day I taught third grade. The students were reading a story about friends. Then they had a discussion about friendship. I told them about you and I being friends for such a long time and how at first when we met I wasn't very kind. I did not give you a friendly welcome to your new neighborhood.

212

During our class discussion the kids gave this summary sentence: "You can be mean to one another at first and still be good friends for a long time," though I don't recommend this approach to friendship.

I guess we are proof of that statement. One of the students asked if I thought you and I would always be friends. I answered, "I am sure of it." Love, Linda

You're in My Yard

During our adult years Patsy made me a beautiful macramé hanging flower basket. She had drilled holes through several chestnuts and entwined the woven braid with chestnuts as decorative pieces. I thought, finally a use for these smooth reddish nuts. I added a flowering basket and hung it on my front porch. Every time I saw those hanging ropes, with the chestnuts I reflected on my childhood memories of gathering these "precious gems" with Patsy.

Innocent Phone Calls

The year 2015 my grandson showed me a video on the computer from "Super Mario Logan Videos." The theme was about these characters making prank phone calls - similar to my real story. So I read the story, "Innocent Phone Calls" to my fifteen-year-old grandson.

Later that evening, I spoke to my older sister and she recalled when she was young, back in the forties, and she and another girlfriend made a prank phone call. They called the only store that was in the town of Gladstone, Oregon and asked if they had Prince Albert in a Can, (Prince Albert was a brand name of a tobacco that was sold in cans.) Then they said, "You should let him out."

My sister told me that at the time she knew it was the wrong thing to do but they didn't get caught. I guess some pranks never fade away.

The Big Production

As an adult I had a job as a Children's Ministry Director. I directed several years of summer Vacation Bible School programs, and two
major Christmas productions. My training began and was basically
limited to my childhood experience of my first big production, The
Talent Show.

Adventure

Years later I relived the adventure story. One afternoon two of my
children were missing. They were ages seven and nine.

Unlike my father, who was about to call the police, I did call the
police. Within the hour an unmarked police car drove up my driveway with two officers and my two daughters.

My girls had decided to follow a helium balloon that was floating
in the sky. As it moved with the wind my children took a tour of our
extended neighborhood and then lost their way back home. I was the
worrying parent rather than the wandering child seeking adventure.

During my college years the "colored issue" didn't matter to me
or to my parents. One of my roommates was a black girl. My parents
accepted and respected her along with her family and her friends.
During one of our college reunions my roommate told me how much
she respected my dad because he treated her kindly. One memory she
shared was a time he fixed her car because it broke down and we were
on our way back to the college. My dad's compassionate, generous
actions always spoke louder than any cautionary words he ever said.

My grade-school friend, Dorothy, was never far from my mind.
I named my favorite doll Dorothy. It was on August 31, 2007 that I
sadly read the obituary notice in the Oregonian. My friend, Dorothy,
had died at the age of sixty-three. I cried over a friendship that didn't
develop because of racial barriers.

You've Got to Be Kidding

I accepted the fact that Pasty's family moved. Marilyn and Nancy were never pleased that when I was thirteen my family moved from NE Portland to SE Portland.

My friends went to Grant High School and after ninth grade I attended Washington High School. I supported a different school, and I cheered the opposing basketball and football teams. Marilyn and Nancy never let me forget that Grant was great and the "best" and it was too bad I had to attend Washington High.

Could This be True?

Camp fire songs stay with you for life. One song that I remember well was called "The Wiener Man." The words went like this: "I know a wiener man he owns a hot dog stand..." Nowadays they would probably change the lyrics to: "I know a Frankfurter Man..." Then, it was an innocent song about a man selling hot dogs.

There are other songs that come to mind from "Kumbaya My Lord" (meaning "Come by here my Lord") to "John Jacob Jingleheimer Schmidt." These tunes bring back wonderful memories of summer campfires at Camp Colton.

What Will I Be When I Grow Up?

In 1965, when I started college, I declared my major as elementary education. I never deviated from that goal. Patsy got the revelation to try teaching much later. In 1969, when Patsy had already graduated from Willamette University with a major in psychology and a minor in German, then she thought about a teaching career.

January 26, 1969

Dear Linda,

I've been giving the matter some serious thought yet I've hesitated to come to any definite conclusion. The other night as I was lying

215

*in bed waiting to go to sleep, it suddenly overcame me. I know
now that's what I want to do. I couldn't go to sleep for a long time
thinking about teaching and praying about it. And of course, more
than anybody, I would like to live with you. I imagine Monmouth
would be the best place to go.*

*If you are considering staying around that area, maybe we could
find an apartment or something else close by. I wouldn't even
mind living some ways a way like in Dallas or Salem.*

*If my opinions have come too late to fit into your plans, that's
all right too because as you know, I'm very flexible! I know that
wherever you choose to go, you will be happy. Love, Patsy*

In January 1969 I was a senior at Oregon College of Education
in Monmouth, Oregon. I loved going to school there and enjoyed the
country side, including the small town atmosphere. My student teaching was at Monmouth Elementary School. I thought having Patsy for
a roommate would be great. My pretend dream was to stay in Monmouth and marry some ideal, young college professor and never leave
this college town.

Fate has a way of changing our dreams. Patsy did not come to
Monmouth. I did not stay there nor did I marry a college professor;
however, we both became teachers.

Nov., 1969

Dear Patsy,

*I am a teacher now with thirty-three third graders to testify to
the fact. It's not quite the utopia situation I had anticipated, but I
must say I've enjoyed 90% of my experience. Every day, despite
the fact that some days are better than others, I've been thankful
that I have this privilege of being a teacher.*

*I am hoping my second year will not be as worrisome, time con-
suming, and blunder-some as this year has been. Love, Linda*

216

September 27, 1985

Dear Linda,

Now I'm teaching Special Ed. classes at the high school. My kids range from 8th grade to 12th grade. I'm teaching full time. I have three Reading, two Writing and one Math class. Discipline is a problem. Most of the kids are boys. I was hired at the last minute. I didn't even know what I would be teaching until the day before school started. You can imagine how busy I've been.

I usually don't even leave the school until midnight. Even on weekends I'm there at least 12 hours a day. Love, Patsy

November 2012

Patsy showed me a box and asked, "Do you remember seeing this?"

I looked at the red and white box with drawings of career people on the cover. Inside the box were ten booklets. It looked familiar. Then I read the title words, "You Can Remember." I couldn't believe it. Patsy still had the complete memory set. I took out the book number one and there were the three associative words and the grocery list.

Year 2015 - According to an October 2012 article in "Country Living Magazine" written by an antiques specialist, Helaine Fendelman, the card game, "Authors" was created in 1861 by a journalist named Anne Abbott. Other game manufacturers produced versions of this game. A complete game with instructions and the original box would be worth $150.

Friday Frolics

I attended other dances, during my high-school years, where I was the "wallflower"- the girl not getting asked to dance. One time was at a live TV Dick Clark show in Portland, Oregon. Another dance was at Seaside. At the time I was in high school. As I remember both times Marilyn and/or Nancy were with me and they got asked to dance.

I felt depressed. After the Seaside dance I came back to the beach cabin and complained to my mother. I told her I wasn't going to curl my hair or do anything to look nice because it didn't matter to the male population anyway.

My mother referred to the example of my dear grandmother, Flora. My grandmother had lost her husband before I was even born. My mom reminded me that Grandma dressed nicely every day, set her hair and always looked attractive. Men were not pursuing her nor did I think she was pursuing them, yet she kept her appearance nice to please herself.

I admired my grandmother and decided to follow her example.

My First Date

When I showed Marilyn and Norman the stories that I had written about our friendship I finally heard about what happened years ago when Norman stopped dating me and asked Marilyn out. Evidently he went to Marilyn's house to visit Earl. Earl had been in an accident and he was at Emmanuel Hospital. Norman asked Marilyn if she would like a ride on his motor scooter to go to the hospital and that was the beginning of their dating.

In July 2010, I visited Marilyn. On her dining room table was a collection of framed photos. One picture was a black and white photo of a young boy age eight and a girl age five. Marilyn told me it was a picture that she didn't even remember but one that her mother had taken years ago. It was a picture of her and Norman. I realized then, for the first time, that Marilyn did not take away my boyfriend; instead when I was in high school I was taking away her boyfriend, though at the time she didn't know Norman was going to be her boyfriend or to be her future husband. In 2015 they celebrated their forty-ninth wedding anniversary.

A Tragic Day

On May 2009 I received a phone call from Norman. He told me Marilyn was in the hospital due to back surgery. She was in "terrible pain." I cried for her again as I did back in February of 1961. Why did Marilyn have to experience so much repeated discomfort?

Then a couple days later I talked to her on the phone. Once again I heard her spirited voice. She was suffering, but I felt she would soon be all right because I knew about upcoming wedding plans. She did fine because within two weeks her daughter got married and Marilyn was at the wedding.

Changes

The other event which caused national sorrow was the fall of the twin towers in New York on September 11, 2001. It was another day when the world felt out of control and the impossible was happening. I knew then that life in America would never be the same and a threat would hang over us as never before.

The Riot

Carl did call Nancy and took her out on a date. Nancy only dated him a couple times and then didn't date him again. Marilyn and I felt horrible that Carl had not asked us out. When we were at the beach he was a wonderful friend to all three of us.

Nancy broke up with Donny,

We shared our wind breaker for years and each year it would be stored at one of our houses. Years later when Marilyn and Norman built a beach house at Rockaway, then we let Marilyn keep the wind breaker. When I visited her in 2010 at a newer beach house in Tillamook, Oregon she showed me old beach towels and the wind breaker that she had saved over the years.

The Seaside Riot of 1962 was the worst outbreak of disturbance in Seaside's history. The National Guard, from nearby Camp Rilea, had to be called by Governor Hatfield to calm the situation. The riot lasted well into the night, at least until 1:00a.m.when the bars closed.

The mob was referred to as, "the rebellious teenagers." The next day there was "still trouble brewing." It is said that music groups helped to calm the kids by playing the popular song, "Louie, Louie" by the Kingsmen, who were at Seaside the night of the riot.

The Storm

Years later my brother, Dan, told me that the night of the storm my father, mother and brother were the last people to cross the Morrison Bridge. Dan said they were closing the bridge lanes because of the extreme wind speed which had reached high gusts of 116 mph.

My dad pleaded with the bridge patrol to let him cross. Dan said it was for the love of his daughter (me) that he was so persistent about wanting to get across town and to check and make sure I was safe.

Final Tallies: forty-six people from Washington or Oregon died during the storm, 53,000 homes were damaged and one million people were without power.

New Church Experiences

On the internet I sadly discovered that Rev. Wendell Wallace passed away in the year 2009. I read that the church, Metropolitan Church of God (where Nancy and I attended years ago) changed location in the year 1967. The congregation moved from the NE corner of Beech and Borthwick to another building on 13th and Skidmore. Skidmore is close to Mason Street where I previously lived. Now the church is called Maranatha Church and the Pastor is Dr. Bethel.

I spoke with Dr. Bethel and he was able to contact the Wallace family. They granted me permission to use the quotes from Rev. Wallace's book for my chapter. I also listened to one of Dr. Bethel's sermons online. He preaches in a similar style as Rev. Wallace. Once again I was inspired and excited hearing the gospel message given in a persuading and vociferous manner.

College Days

Throughout my teaching career I took college courses to gain credits so I could renew my certificate. I received more than ninety-eight post-college credits. I had an elementary teaching certificate and a special education endorsement. A college degree was not the end of my studies.

Sometimes the circle of life revolves and repeats history. On August 21, 2015 a cartoon movie titled, "The Prophet" will be introduced to the public. This film is from the book, "The Prophet" by Kahlil Gibran. The same book that Patsy and I shared during our college years.

Gibran's book has never gone out of print and has sold over a million copies. Now its popularity will be appreciated by the youth of today - amazing.

A Bad Idea

There are similarities to the earthquake of 1949 and the one of 1965. Both of these quakes originated from the Juan de Fuca Plate and the North American Plate. The quake of 1949 was a magnitude 7.1 and the one of 1965 was a magnitude 6.5. They both did similar damage and in some places damage to the same buildings.

The tsunami that we were waiting for in March 1964 did reach certain shorelines and some people died from the ocean activity. The greatest death toll was along the Gulf of Alaska. There were also four people who drowned from high waves in Newport Bay, Oregon during that same time frame.

It wasn't until 2004 when I watched on television the devastation of the tsunami of Indonesia and then later in 2011 the tsunami of Japan that I realized that our youthful experience of trying to be where disaster might strike was foolish. I've been fortunate to only experience minor quakes without major loss.

Indecision

The year (2015) I asked Patsy how she felt now (years after her indecision day) about not continuing on her mission with the Peace Corps. Here is her answer: "I wasn't clear as to what my life path was to be. But, I have no regrets. I love everything I have done. I have taken life moment by moment, one step at a time. Maybe the Peace Corps was too big of a commitment for me at the time. That's okay. I aimed for the stars by wanting to go into the Peace Corps. Good for me! The training was a great experience! But I am who I am, and I accept myself, and I know that everything has worked out the way it was meant to be. I really believe that we all do the best we can with what we have at the time. I didn't go into the Peace Corps, but I did travel and did other jobs instead, and I think those are the things I really needed to do in my life. So it's all good."

Central Oregon

During the year 1966-1967 Patsy went back to college and completed a medical technology program. In the fall of 1967 she purchased a '56 Chevy and took her dog, Jack, and headed east - beyond Oregon. Georgia was her first long-term stop.

School Struggles

Years later I was the teacher and not the student. During one incident I was not satisfied with a student's essay. He wrote about his summer vacation and basically said he did nothing, but watch TV. I told him if he could go one week without watching TV and then re-write his paper explaining what he did during that week then I would give him a higher grade than what he would receive otherwise, and I would give him a five dollar bill.

I put a five dollar bill in my desk drawer. He eliminated television watching for one week and handed me his rewritten assignment. I smiled and handed him his reward.

A Desperate Call in the Amazon

It is the year 2015 I called Nancy to talk to her about this story. She said she remembered the day as if it were yesterday, but she is unsure of the name of the falls and thinks it could be the falls called Boquerón de Padre Abad. She added that during the night there was a deluge of water that started coming into their tents so it was a "real eventful day."

I told her that I had watched several YouTube videos on the area of Yarinachocah and even now (years from when she was there) the land looks remote, poor and like a jungle. One website is called: lonelyplanet.com/peru. In each video that I observed the words were in Spanish with Spanish music in the background. Despite the bareness of the land and the roughness of the roads or lack thereof, the people appeared happy. Nancy said it was like that when she was there - if asked, they would answer with one word that meant they were "content."

The summer Institute of Linguistics celebrated sixty years of service during the year 2006. At that time the linguists had assisted with documenting sixty-eight Peruvian languages.

I'm sure Nancy was helpful when she was in her twenties and on this mission trip. When I took high school Spanish she was a main source of help. I would call her on the phone and ask her to pronounce the words for me. She had a natural talent for foreign languages.

It is July 23, 2015 and tonight I received a copy of a letter that Nancy sent back in August 1977. Nancy spent ten months in Peru on her mission assignment. This is an excerpt of her letter from Peru.

Greetings from Peru

Much to my surprise, I was asked to accompany one of our linguists to visit the Taushiro tribe located just south of the Ecuador border. The purpose of the ten day trip was to see how the Taushirors were doing since we have no way of communicating with them where they are located. They are a remote group of people who have been victimized by dreadful epidemics and cruelties of jungle life down through the years. Years ago they were a large tribe, but now only twelve Taushiros remain.

We left the base and traveled 350 miles north by float plane, we landed at the nearest body of water, the Tigre River. After parting with our pilot, we spent a few nights on the river preparing for our all-day canoe trip to see this tribe of people. Canoe is the only way to reach these people. My partner, Tali, and I traveled in a dug-out (with a small motor) for eleven hours non-stop. The stream that took us to the Taushiros is a remote as you can imagine and it was necessary for us to literally cut a path for ourselves as the underbrush was so thick. Along the way we saw the most fantastic scenery I've ever seen as well as monkeys swinging from trees, and huge flocks of Macaws. Wild life in that region is abundant. Prior to our arrival at the tribe, a large tiger was killed. The danger of the surrounding wild life is one of the reasons there are around 45-50 dogs at the tribe with only 12 people.

My first meal was monkey and toucan. Yum, yum! They would have been tastier if I hadn't seen them brought home fresh from the hunt and then prepared step by step ready to eat. My favorite meal out of all the things we had (large rodents, Macaws etc.) was wild boar.

I was constantly reminded of Psalm 67: 5, 7 "Praise God, O world: May all the peoples of the earth give thanks to you... and peoples from remotest lands will worship Him." It doesn't get anymore remote than where we were!

Added note: From reading on line, I discovered that one of the families that Nancy stayed with while in Peru has since died from illness. The only family member that is still alive is a man named Amadao Garcia. He is the only person alive that still knows the Taushiro (also called Pinche, Pinchi) language as of 2008. Also the name Neftail Alicea (Tali) is listed on Wikipedia as the only person that studied their language back in the seventies. This is the same gal that went with Nancy years ago to visit this tribe of people and study their language.

Website: Toptenz listed Taushiro as the top rarest language spoken in the world.

Fate or Plans

At the close of the letter that I wrote to Patsy I added news of what Marilyn and Nancy were doing in the year 1969. News wise: Nancy quit working at Youth for Christ and now she is with a tour group in California singing at different places. Next she is going to visit missions in Mexico.

Marilyn and Norm married in the year 1969 and then went to live in New York. Norm is completing his doctorate degree in law.

It was years later on a cold winter day when I reread this invitation from Patsy to join her at the Cloister Hotel. I looked up the

Cloister Hotel on the internet. What a beautiful place! I thought if this invitation came again I would find a way to go.

Lies

There was another lie during this time of my life. It wasn't a lie I told - it was a lie Ron told when we first started dating.

It sent a message to me, like a warning light, and it should have stopped our relationship. I was already wanting him and wanting him to be everything that I hoped for in a relationship. The warning did not change my path of falling in love.

Ron had promised me that he had quit smoking. I did not approve of his smoking habit. I was upset to see him smoke, but I was more concerned that he told me he had quit and obviously he hadn't. My immediate thought was he lied to me.

The Secret

In later years Marilyn had a stillborn baby. She told me the sad news via phone when I was living in Minnesota. She and Norman adopted two more children.

Over the years I had two children, experienced one miscarriage and then had two more children. My child birth experiences were quicker and easier than Marilyn's descriptions. For my third birth I was rushed to the hospital by ambulance and once I reached the hospital my baby was born within fifteen minutes.

The Argument

It was because of Marilyn's strong character that she was able to meet the battles that life threw at her over the years. I never knew Marilyn to be anything but a fighter and to keep herself up and going no matter what the circumstances. She has always been a loyal friend to me despite any of our personality differences. After this disagreement about my lack of helping at the beach house, there was never a doubt about our friendship. It really didn't matter if we agreed or disagreed. It was mutually understood that our friendship would continue.

Differences

It is amazing, but when I finally did take a trip to Hawaii (eighteen years later in 1998) the first place Patsy took me was to a McDonald's. By then she was living in a rental house in Hilo. I doubt that she remembered my comment from the letter I had written those previous years. She instinctively knew what I really liked and wanted to make sure I had a satisfying stay.

A Walk on the Beach

On November 24, 2009 Roland (Ron) McCoy died from lung cancer. It was a sudden yet horrible death and I grieved. I was sorrowful over past hopes and dreams that we did not achieve. I grieved because my grown kids were in grief and rushed to their dying father's bedside in California. I was miles away in Washington. Ron had remarried so California was not the place nor was it the time for me (his ex-wife) to be any part of the mourning rituals. It had been years since I was part of Ron's life, but I still felt the pain of losing a man that I once deeply loved.

A Hawaii Visit

While in Hawaii in 1998 I saw many sights that Patsy had mentioned to me years before. We hiked through the area of Akaka Falls, from a high cliff we saw the wilderness of Waipio Valley, and we spent one afternoon touring the Volcano National Park.

California Reunion

Marilyn and Nancy did not get to witness a future trip I experienced at Disneyland where I did ride all the rides except for the giant roller coaster. I went with my daughter to Disneyland in the year 2014. Our trip to Disneyland was the day after I had ridden with my daughter on her Kawasaki motorcycle on the freeway in California. After that experience I had no fear of the controlled Disneyland rides; even my claustrophobic feelings diminished, for that day at least. Too bad Marilyn wasn't there to see my bravery.

A Sunny Day

Rod and I enjoyed Willow Grove and often went to walk on the path or sometimes sit in the car and watch the ships go by. We also liked going to the Oregon coast. There we walked along the prom and shopped in the stores. We had a beach theme in our family room and some paintings on the wall that we had purchased from the beach.

So in the year 2014 I went to Seaside with my daughter, step-daughter and my step-grandson and there we distributed my late husband's ashes on the sand and in the ocean waves. It was a place that I knew Rod loved and the beach that gave me fond, peaceful memories.

California Visit - 2013

My daughter's motorcycle accident mentioned in this story was not to be her last accident. On July 6, 2014 while at work driving a motorcycle up a truck ramp she had another major accident. Somehow the motorcycle did not make a safe transfer from ramp to the back of the truck. Danita and the motorcycle slid off the ramp. Miraculously only part of the motorcycle landed on her. She was injured with three broken bones in her vertebrae, but she did recover.

Hawaii Second Time

In August 2014 a hurricane Iselle hit the Puna area where Patsy lives. Numerous Albizia trees fell damaging homes and blocking roadways. Patsy had no home damage, but along with many others she was without power for several days. She told me one concern everyone had was finding ice to help keep their foods cold.

My daughter and I were at Safeway and as a fun uplift for Patsy we sent her a picture of us standing in front of an ice cabinet full of packaged ice. Then we added a note saying if she wanted ice, come to Washington.

She sent this e-mail message back. "I just turned on my cell phone and received your picture of ice and your message. Oh, that was the sweetest thing! Look at all that ice! And you are so proudly displaying it, telling me it could all be mine if I only moved there. How clever! How true! I laughed and laughed!"

Then in October 2014 there was concern for a lava flow from Mt. Kilauea within four miles of Patsy's home. It took months of flowing slowly across several areas, but did not head in the direction of where Patsy lives.

An Honest Man

The Bible verifies Marilyn's encouraging words: Revelation 21:4: "God will remove all of their sorrows, and there will be no death or sorrow or crying or pain."

I Corinthians 15:42-43: "Our earthly bodies, which die and decay, will be different when they are resurrected, for they will never die. Our bodies now disappoint us, but when they are raised, they will be full of glory. They are weak now, but when they are raised, they will be full of power."

Before Rod died he was given recognition of his years of loyal service for the Department of Social Health Services. His department dedicated a foster visitation room in his honor. There is a plaque on the wall recognizing his services. Now (close to three years after his death) my daughter Selena is working in the same building where Rod worked. Often her duties involve visitation supervision in the same room that was dedicated to Rod's memory. It is amazing how fate intervenes in our lives.

READERS' GROUP GUIDE

Childhood Years

1. Tell about a positive or negative school experience.
2. Do you have any friends who have extremely different likes than your interests?
3. Tell about a science experiment you tried and explain the results.
4. Share about a time you started a project, but then your parents or another person stopped you from completing your efforts or helped you to complete the project.
5. Despite their differences what do Marilyn and Linda have in common that seals their friendship?
6. Have you had the experience of meeting someone and at first misjudging them and then later discovering they were different than your first impression?
7. Why is it so hard to meet a new friend?
8. How are children entertaining themselves today? Name some positive creative activities you know that they do.
9. From the story, The Unwelcomed Greeting, why do you think Linda had a hard time greeting Patsy?
10. Who is your best friend and why does your friendship work?

Teenage Years

1. Tell about your first date.
2. Was high school easy or hard for you and why?
3. How do you think students are dealing with social skills today and how can we help them?
4. How old were you when you decided what career you wanted to pursue - did you follow that goal?
5. What are some ways we can help young students today to select career options?

6. Did you grow up in the same house for years or did your family move from place to place and how did you feel about the stability or the changes?
7. What are your feelings now about the career choices you made or are making?
8. Have you had similar experiences as these girls did during the Columbus Day Storm or the Seaside Riot?
9. Did you experience youth mission trips or scout group trips that influenced your life?
10. Name the educational or training courses you have completed for credit or enjoyment

College Years

1. Tell about two important decisions you made during your college years or during your early twenties.
2. What did you do after completing high school?
3. Which story so far in the book have you related to or enjoyed the most and why?
4. Have you ever experienced a time when you had a major decision, as Patsy did, when you had to weigh the options and how did you feel afterwards?
5. Have you ever been in a fearful situation as Nancy experienced and what was the outcome?
6. Tell about Peace Corps or missionary experiences that you are familiar with and how they influenced your life or someone's life you know.
7. What opportunities did you have as a youth that you took advantage of or that you were unable to accept?
8. Is studying still part of your life and if so what subjects or interests are you pursuing?
9. What challenges are college students facing today and how can we help?
10. Tell about a friend you knew in college that helped with your studies or were you the helping friend?

Adult Years

1. What lie has been part of your life that you are willing to share?
2. After The Argument chapter discuss how Linda and Marilyn are different and why they still maintain friendship.
3. Tell about a "stormy" friendship that you've maintained.
4. What are some ways to establish family times, but also to include friends?
5. Do you think it is important for women to have women friends and men to have men friends a part from their spouses and why?
6. Why is forgiveness so important among friends?
7. Tell about a trip you've had with an adult friend.
8. Tell about a time you had an argument with a friend and how it did or did not get resolved.
9. List reasons why friends are important.
10. List three aspects that characterize a true friend.